A handsome wall plaque modeled in low relief on foil, adapted from a weathervane.

foilcraft

CYRIL MARSHALL

STACKPOLE BOOKS

FOILCRAFT
Copyright © 1977 by
Cyril Leek Marshall

Published by
STACKPOLE BOOKS
Cameron and Kelker Streets
P.O. Box 1831
Harrisburg, Pa. 17105

Published simultaneously in Don
Mills, Ontario, Canada
by Thomas Nelson & Sons, Ltd.

Library of Congress Cataloging in Publication Data

Marshall, Cyril Leek, 1906-
  Foilcraft.
  Bibliography: p.
  Includes index.
  1. Metal-work.   2. Metal foils.   I. Title.
TT205.M32 1977   745.56   77-7573
ISBN O-8117-0647-8 *Mar*

Printed in the U.S.A.

TO TOUMA
and all others
who have
inspired me

Contents

71 . . Chapter 3—More Advanced Foil Projects

89 . . Chapter 4—Fundamentals of Foil Sculpture

PART II: Advanced Metalcraft

97 . . Chapter 5—Duplicating Foil Components

Contents

10

Contents

11

ACKNOWLEDGMENTS

Looking back over more than half a century as a practicing artist-craftsman, it would be impossible to name all those who in some way contributed to my ability to work with my hands or inspired me to creative effort. There were those who taught me the rudiments of art, and others who taught me craft skills that gave me a livelihood.

Thus armed, I came to America from England in the years of the deep depression and managed to survive, and at the same time picked up new skills, out of necessity. During World War II the American Navy made use of my artistic skills to produce training manuals. At war's end I became a teacher of the young, instructing in arts and crafts. The last twenty years of fulltime employment were spent in the museum field, a challenge to all of my skills. Upon retirement I turned to writing, and thanks to several editors and a receptive publisher, I have been given an opportunity to pass on some of my knowledge of crafts.

I owe thanks to the Metropolitan Museum of Art in New York for photographs of valuable antique repoussé work, and to the Dumbarton Oaks Collection for pictures of pre-Columbian Indian foilwork. All remaining photographs, except as otherwise noted, are by Ted Avery of Kingston, Massachusetts, who worked long and patiently with lights and camera.

I owe thanks to those companies that made their products available to me for testing, namely, the Devcon Corporation of Danvers, Massachusetts, makers of Devcon epoxy and specialty products; and the Brookstone Company of Peterborough, New Hampshire, and National Camera, of Englewood, Colorado, both of which sent me materials or tools to test, as well as useful photographs.

Finally, I wish to thank friends who encouraged me in my work, including my wife, who so often left me undisturbed in my studio, and at other times urged me to new efforts when book writing seemed less than the ideal pastime.

INTRODUCTION

As a creative medium, metal foils have been used for thousands of years in both the Old World and the New World, with examples to be found in great museums everywhere. Columbus brought back incredibly beautiful and skillfully made work by the misnamed Indians of Central America, much of it decorated with fine granules of gold, a technique unknown to the goldsmiths of Europe at that time. It was not until the year 1930 that an Englishman named Littleton working for the British Museum discovered it, but the secret of how these Indians converted ores into metal foils remains a mystery to this day.

The early discoverers of metals, because of the difficulties encountered in converting ores into workable quantities, were forced to use them sparingly. For this reason they beat them, by unknown means, into thin sheets we now call foil. In this form it was easily deformed, but by a process known as embossing, some rigidity was given to it. The tools used for this purpose are unknown, but it is presumed they were of wood.

Piercing as a means of decoration was common, and examples of ritual masks having openings for eyes and mouth have been dug from ancient sites. The nose, modeled separately, was inserted in an opening cut for that purpose. Most of this early work was in gold, a metal that was also hammered so thin it could be used as gilding for ornaments on buildings and furniture. Such ornamentation was applied with a glue size.

With time came the mastery of metal forging and casting, along with a means of rolling metal to gauges thicker than foil. The techniques of producing relief decoration on metal, called repoussé, made use of hammers and punches, and work in this medium flourished during the Renaissance. Work was done in such high relief that it was difficult to distin-

13

guish from castings, except by means of its lighter weight. The smiths used similar techniques to decorate suits of armor for those who could afford them.

The metalwork of the past should be an inspiration to the worker in foils, and while it is not possible with foil to obtain the degree of relief of repoussé, it is quite easy to achieve what might be called instant forms of that technique, using tools of wood much like those of our ancestors.

The modeler's terms for the amount of relief desired are *high* and *low,* the former meaning that ornamentation or figures are modeled almost in the round, away from the background. *Low* relief is slightly raised, with no undercutting of the ornaments or figures. The foil modeler uses low relief.

Some crafts such as paper sculpture and découpage, both of which demand some skill with knife and scissors, have interchangeable techniques and tools. The same skills used in working with paper are also used in cutting and forming foils.

The serious craftsperson, jeweler, decorator, frame maker, and designer can use foils to translate ideas into three-dimensional forms, the better to evaluate them. In fact, good design and accurate layout are both important considerations in foilcraft, sometimes calling for a knowledge of geometry and the development of solids, both subjects to be covered in the text.

It should not be expected that a writer could solve all the problems that may arise in the practice of a given craft; however, the reader may benefit from the experience of the author, one who served an apprenticeship with an English company of art metalworkers, later in America branching into other fields including designing for industry, teaching crafts, and creating museum exhibits.

To the uninitiated, foil is a material used for packaging or in the kitchen, as freezer wrap or an aid to cooking. Many people have no knowledge of the various foils used for craftwork, or what may be accomplished with them.

Considerably heavier in weight than household foil, the metal used in foilcraft is still quite light, and is easily worked using simple tools. Its surface may be modeled in low relief or it may be kept perfectly smooth and flat. With some very basic knowledge about geometric figures and their construction, it may even be cut and assembled into nearly any shape desired, producing metal sculpture.

14

Foilcraft lends itself well to many decorative purposes:

- To cover lampshades, picture frames, waste baskets, cans, or bottles, and to upgrade any number of commonplace articles
- To cover door panels and cabinets, in either plain or modeled form
- For mirror surrounds and as decoration on glass
- To make or decorate clock dials
- For reflective backing of candle sconces
- To make lanterns and candleholders
- As decoration on trays, canisters, and boxes
- For creating jewelry in wide variety
- To cover napkin rings or holders
- For decorative wall plaques and replicas of weathervanes
- To make signs and cut-out letters
- For small sculptures, toys, miniatures, and party decorations
- For enameling (copper foil) to produce jewelry, dishes, and ornaments
- As a means for designers to better visualize their work in an extra dimension
- To form decorative and utilitarian shapes by spinning over forms in a lathe

Foil as a decorative medium is limited only by the imagination, and may be used plain or modeled in a wide variety of forms.

It is hoped others will be inspired to try their hands at foilcraft.

Part I

WORKING
WITH
METAL FOILS

Chapter 1

MATERIALS, EQUIPMENT, AND DESIGN

When contemplating the practice of an unfamiliar craft, first consider the potential afforded as a medium for self-expression. Investigate also the skills required for its performance, the materials and processes involved, and the tools and equipment required in its practice.

The foils are available in a variety of metals and finishes, and the additional materials are inexpensive, and can be obtained in most hardware stores. The tools for getting started are few and simple, costing less than for those of most other crafts. Additional tools may be acquired if deemed necessary, or to speed up work; power tools are optional. Some form of workbench or table is a necessity. The few chemicals used are common and low in cost.

FOILS

Defined, foils are metals rolled to very thin gauges, conforming to Brown and Sharpe's standards laid down for the wire and metal trades (see Appendix). The scale runs from 6/0-gauge (.5800 inches) to 44-gauge (.001978 inches), with the foils ranging from 33- to 38-gauge. For most craft work foil is available in gauges from 34 through 38, and comes in 24-, 18- and 12-inch widths, in rolls up to 25 feet, with even longer rolls for school and industrial use.

Metals available are copper, brass, and aluminum, the latter in silver, gold, red, blue, and green, and matt or smooth finishes; the reverse side of the colored foils is silver. Foils of lead and tin are mostly used in packaging, and are seldom seen in craft supply outlets.

Foils of precious metals are sold by karat weight, and are expensive, being used primarily in the jewelry trade. Household aluminum foils which come in light and heavy grades (the gauges of which are not listed on the package), are also used for special projects.

CHARACTERISTICS OF VARIOUS FOILS

Although all the foils mentioned can be modeled, copper and brass are superior for the purpose, one reason being that they take on added rigidity when modeled with metal tools. Aluminum does not so respond, and because of the surface finishes, wooden tools should be used when working this metal. Copper has one other advantage in that it can be enameled at a temperature that would melt brass or aluminum. The latter metals may be decorated by using pseudo-enamels made from plastics.

ADDING RIGIDITY TO FOIL

In addition to embossing foil to give it added stiffness, early craftsmen sometimes backed it with wax, pitch, or some other plastic substance. There is no reason why these same materials should not be used today except that, thanks to modern technology, there are even better substances available for the purpose. So-called powder metallurgy has spawned a great many side benefits other than its use to replace the casting of metal parts. The powdered metals—steel, bronze, aluminum, and others—are mixed with self-hardening pastes to make "liquid" solders, auto body filler materials, and the like, many of which can be put to use as backing materials and fillers. These pastes are packed in tubes and sold in hardware stores.

Kiln-fired Enamels

Enamels come in both soft- and hard-fire enamels, and in transparent as well as opaque colors in a wide range. Enameling is the best method of stiffening copper foil because it must be coated on both sides to prevent warping. A kiln is required, the least expensive of which is about thirty dollars. Should the desire be to keep the metallic look of the foil, just two enamels would serve: A clear flux that when fired gives the copper a gold look, and counter enamel, for use on the back of a piece. Both are made to adhere to the foil with the aid of a special gum and are fired at the same time (see Chapter 8). Both are available at craft supply outlets.

Pseudo-Enamels and Plastic Fillers

If the use of a kiln is impractical, there are several other materials that can be used to simulate enamels. These are plastic powders or crystals which fire in a kitchen oven at 350 degrees Fahrenheit, and are available in a good range of colors. Un-Namels are of the powder type, the others are known as Cooking Crystals. A third method called Boss-Gloss uses paste colors mixed with an activator. This offers good control, but takes longer to do and to set up hard. With it finer work can be done. Full directions come with all these products.

Wood Fillers

A fairly new product is Elmer's wood filler, an improvement over the older plastic wood, which tends to shrink away from surfaces to which it is applied. The new type dries more slowly, and will adhere to almost any kind of surface, including metal. It does not shrink, and can be applied directly from the tube in which it is packed. This is an excellent, though opaque, material for backing.

Metal Fillers

There are many types of plastic metals and putties, the putties much used in auto body shops for filling dents. These materials set up (harden) rapidly unless first thinned with acetone, in which case they can be brushed on for a neater effect. Devcon and Duro are two good brands, and there are also Lab-Metal and Sculp-Metal, the latter being available in various metal-matching colors. This type of stiffener is applied to the back of a sculptured or modeled piece, to help prevent denting.

Liquid Plastics

There are several liquid plastics that are used for embedment of scientific specimens and in the making of costume jewelry, which can be used to stiffen a piece of modeled foil if it is dished around its edges to contain the plastic in its liquid stage. A whole piece may be embedded, but this is not always desirable. These embedment materials need to be activated by use of a hardener, a few drops per ounce being sufficient. Pour the liquid to a depth of not more than ⅜-inch in the mold, and let it jell before either placing the object to be embedded or adding to the depth. When set, the plastic is hard, and can be finished easily by polishing with a rouged buffing wheel. When its use is permissible, this is a satisfactory medium for stiffening foil, because it is clear and does not hide the natural beauty of the metal.

Plaster of Paris and Crack-filling Materials

If a piece of modeled foil is to be applied to a background or glued to a round or rectangular object, there is need only to fill the modeled parts from the back, and for this there are several inexpensive materials that can be used, such as plaster of paris, or the crack-filling compounds, powdered or in paste form. The Ancients made use of pitch or wax, and these too are satisfactory, even though a trifle messy to use.

The crack-fillers, include, among others, Durham's Water Putty and a Canadian product called Polyfilla. These do not shrink when dry, as plaster does.

Glue as Backing

Old-fashioned carpenter's glue may be used, but it too is difficult to apply, and has a bad odor. The newer hot-melt glues are better and easier to use. They are applied with a special electrically heated gun, set to a cream color, and become quite hard. This glue is useful as a filler but not for applying foil to a surface, because it sets up fast and would be difficult to spread evenly.

Solder as Backing

Copper and brass foils may be given a backing of soft solder to stiffen them. This is done by use of a gas torch or soldering iron. Metal to be soldered must be clean and free from grease; the cleaning can be done by abrasive methods, or by dipping in an acid solution. A product called Sparex II (a powdered acid-substitute) when dissolved in water makes a good metal cleaner.

To coat the foil with solder, its surface is heated with a torch until hot enough to melt the solder. Some solders are manufactured with a flux core (resin and acid cores are available), to make them flow more easily.

Apply a good coat of solder, being careful not to overspill onto the front surface, as it is difficult to remove any excess. A 1/16-inch coating is ample to stiffen the foil. Any overspill will have to be removed by abrasion, and this means that the whole front surface will then have to be refinished.

This process may also be accomplished with a soldering iron, preferably of the electric type. Using an iron, it is easier to deposit solder in depressions, without also covering the flat areas. This is ideal if the foil is to be mounted or needs to be bent into shape in any way.

Other Ways to Add Strength

There are mechanical ways to strengthen foils, such as by mounting them on a stiffer background of metal, wood, or plastic. Frames made of wood, brass angle, or lead (as used for stained glass), also act as stiffeners, but modeled areas may still have to be stiffened by one of the filler methods, to prevent denting of the raised ornament.

A piece of jewelry may need only to be framed in some way, because it usually gets gentle handling. This is also true of a large piece intended for hanging on a wall.

Use dictates the type of stiffening needed.

SUITABLE GLUES

The best all-around glue for the foil worker is an all-purpose type, of which there are several. Weldbond is one of the better ones. (Elmer's glue, though good for many craft uses, is *not* suitable for use on metal; it is for porous materials.) The so-called "miracle" glues, while useful for spot gluing, are too expensive and tricky to use for overall gluing.

For foil applied to an object, it is not always necessary to glue other than the ends where the foil meets, and for this purpose the epoxy glues are best. These come in two tubes on a card, one of which is a hardener to be mixed in equal parts with the resin before application. Such joints should be held together by elastic bands until set, to make a very tight joint. Duco cement may be used for this same purpose, but it is not as strong as epoxy.

The contact cements grab on contact, and are difficult to use without help in positioning parts to be cemented. Moreover, unless the foil goes on smoothly, any ripples or bubbles are impossible to remove.

The silicone pastes, usually used in a caulking gun, may be used if evenly spread over a surface on which foil is to be mounted. While these pastes are useful as a glue, they may also act as a filler for modeled foil, although they never get truly hard, being of a rubbery consistency.

Touch-N-Glue is a good adhesive for making joints in foils but would be hard to apply overall. The worker in foils should experiment with various fillers and glues to find those best suited to specific needs.

Knowledge gained through experience with a wide variety of products is passed on here, and any product that is mentioned favorably can be trusted to do the task as outlined.

FINISHES FOR FOILCRAFT

Most foils do not need to be finished after being worked on, except that both brass and copper are susceptible to a wide range of coloration and surface changes. The colored aluminum foils may be modified to some degree, and surface finishes can be removed with acetone should this be desirable for a special effect of contrast. Products to be used as finishes for brass and copper are listed in the Appendix, and have been tested and used by craftsmen, some having been used for centuries. Abrading and polishing is accomplished by the use of pumice, emery or carborundum powders, or by the use of tripoli and rouge on the polishing wheel. These techniques will seldom be needed for foils other than brass and copper. Both these may be quickly toned by the use of liver of sulphur, which turns the metals black or brown, depending on the strength of the solution. Highlighting for contrast may then be achieved by rubbing the surface of the foil with fine steel wool.

TOOLS AND PREPARATIONS

Because working drawings are so important the tools first needed are at the head of the list. This does not mean an investment is necessary in an expensive set of drawing instruments as the type used in schools will serve well. As a matter of fact, they may be better, as in the case of the compass, which will take either pencil or knife.

Some of the tools are shown in figure 1, and are numbered.

drawing board
steel-bladed T-square (no. 13)
adjustable triangle (no. 4)
two types of compass (nos. 5 and 6)
beam compass (no. 3)
Euclid Glide Rule (no. 14)

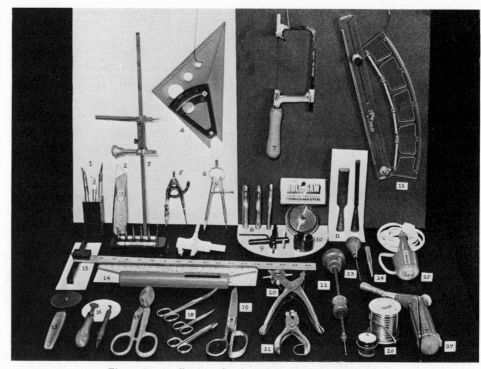

Figure 1. A collection of tools useful to the foilcraft worker.

Acu-Arc for curves (no. 12)
protractor
tracing and drawing papers
pencils and eraser
15-inch steel rule
Slide-Comp (new type of compass)
pens and ink (optional)
lining pen or felt-tip pen (optional)
adhesive tape (to secure drawings)
transfer carbon paper

Numbers 12 and 14, and the Slide-Comp are useful professional tools that, while optional, will help speed up work and insure accuracy.

WORK AREA

A proper workbench with two working levels and a series of drawers for tools is ideal, but a drafting table can also serve well for working with foils. If neither is feasible, plastic trays can be purchased from variety stores to hold tools so that they may be easily seen and selected for use. If the work area is one such as a card table that must be put away after each use, a small toolbox is suggested to hold all gear.

As a working surface, corrugated cardboard is a good general-purpose material, but for different types of modeling, experimentation with various materials is the only way to decide what backup material is best in order to achieve the desired indentation.

BASIC TOOLS

Some of the tools needed for modeling and working with foils, appear in figure 1, and others are in figure 2. Because the first thing to do is cut foil from a roll, either a sharp knife (no. 2) or a pair of shears (nos. 17 and 19) is needed. A large paper cutter that will take the width of the roll may be used. The other knives shown (no. 1) are useful for cutting where scissors cannot reach (for interior cuts).

The Slide-Comp and beam compass (no. 3) are useful for cutting circles of foil, with a knife replacing the pencil. A pair of curved and a pair of straight scissors, small, will be needed as in number 18. The steel-bladed T-square (no. 13) is used when cutting foil with a knife. The cut should always be made on the outside of a design, so that if the knife slips, the design will still be intact.

Figure 2 shows the basic tools used for modeling foil. These shapes come in several sizes. At the top are spoon tools used with forefinger in the bowl when modeling large areas. (The smaller of the two once served to stir a highball, but is now useful for another purpose.) There are other shapes of the same tool that can be picked up for use, some with ball ends.

The wedge- and chisel-shaped tools are for getting into corners and tight places. The tool with the saw-tooth end is for texturing foil, using a scribbling motion for allover pattern, and straight for a striated surface. The ball-ended tools serve several purposes: for indenting, or for making straight lines common to borders. They may also be used for "dimpling" or raising domes in the foil.

At the bottom of figure 2 is shown a dapping die and punch for making domes, a process that will be described more fully later. In figure 1, beneath the beam compass (no. 3) is a set of X-Acto tools used for modeling leather. These same tools can be used to model brass and copper foil, but not aluminum, which should be worked only with wooden tools.

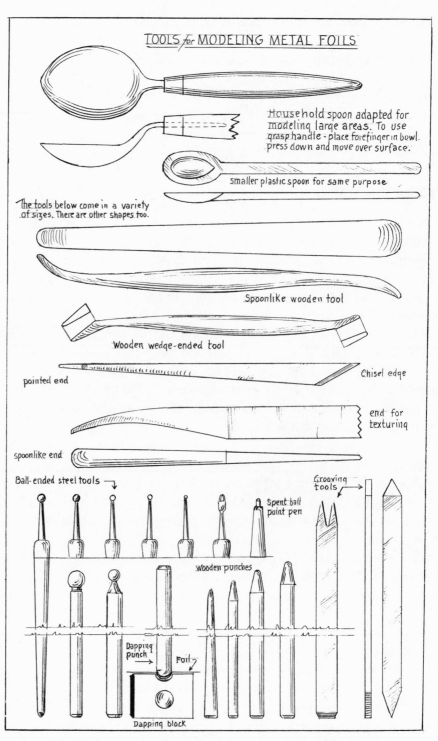

TOOLS for MODELING METAL FOILS

Household spoon adapted for modeling large areas. To use grasp handle - place forefinger in bowl. press down and move over surface.

smaller plastic spoon for same purpose

The tools below come in a variety of sizes. There are other shapes too.

Spoonlike wooden tool

Wooden wedge-ended tool

pointed end

Chisel edge

end for texturing

spoonlike end

Ball-ended steel tools

Spent ball point pen

Grooving tools

Wooden punches

Dapping punch

Foil

Dapping block

Figure 2.

OPTIONAL TOOLS

Outside of the basic tools there may be a need for others. When the occasion arises for making holes in foil, be the need practical or ornamental, there are several tools to choose from. For small holes, a gimlet (fig. 1, no. 23) will serve, but it does make jagged edges on the back of the pierced metal. A better tool for small holes is the hand drill (no. 22) used with drill bits. Larger holes may be made with punches (no. 8), which range in size from ¼-inch to ½-inch, and are used in leather working, as is the rotary punch (no. 20), graded from 3/64- to 3/16-inch; some have extra punches up to ¼-inch. The paper punch (no. 21) makes a ¼-inch hole.

If even larger holes are to be cut, there are tools for that purpose. Two are shown in figure 1, numbers 9 and 10; the tool at left is a wing cutter, adjustable from ⅞-inch to 4 inches. At right, the nested hole saws are graded from ⅞-inch to 2¼ inches. A word of warning on the use of these devices: They will not cut only one sheet of foil unless it is mounted between two sheets of hardboard with edges taped to hold the foil in place. If multiple cutting is to be done, these are the tools to use.

If disks are the objective, the hole saws are unsuitable, because the center drill makes a hole as the tool revolves. For disks use a compass with a knife mounted in place of the pencil. Use the beam compass for large disks. To be free of a center hole, tape a piece of card at the center of the circle to accept the compass point.

For rectangular holes use a knife or a chisel (no. 12); for curved holes a gouge will serve.

Straight-sided hole cutting is a somewhat simple matter, but there are also times when foil must be removed from internal, relatively intricate parts of a design. This cannot often be accomplished with fine scissors; therefore a knife must be used. An X-Acto pointed blade is best for this operation, but when cutting thin card under the same conditions, a round-ended blade works better, and does not tear or make a ragged line.

The center punch (no. 24) is used to make a mark before drilling or, in some cases, to punch a hole. Number 25 is a vibrating tool used for writing names or numbers on tools, which can be useful in texturing operations, mostly on metal thicker than foil.

Number 27 is a gas torch for soldering, and number 26 designates the solder and flux used in this operation.

Three sizes of marking-off tools are numbers 15 and 16, the largest of which is borrowed from the kitchen. The smaller ones are used to prick holes in paper on which a design is drawn so that when pounced with chalk, it is transferred to the work. When making a row of domes along a line, as in a border, the wheeled tool marks their center point, on which a doming tool is placed and tapped, thus assuring an even border. The tools described or even fewer are sufficient equipment to proceed with the modeling and working of metal foils.

DESIGN AND BALANCE

It cannot be over-emphasized that good design and working drawings are vital to the success of any project undertaken, whether simple or more advanced. Students soon learn to make their own designs instead of copying those of others once they grasp a few basic principles.

Every object used in daily life, be it house, automobile, or even a spoon, requires first a design, then a working drawing before it can be produced, and the designers quite likely studied basic design as a foundation of their education. Even those who believe they have no creative ability may have at one time or another indulged in doodling, or played with a compass making circles and arcs into crude patterns. These forms are basic in design, as a study of art history will reveal.

THE IMPORTANCE OF PROPORTION

The Greeks long ago evolved the "golden mean" or perfect proportion basic to good architecture, and they were aware of the fact that the human eye, observing two parallel lines, as the two sides of a perpendicular column, would see them more correctly if they were gradually tapered as they rose. This optical trick they called *entasis*. Similarly, when a statue was to be placed high, the sculptor made the top of the figure larger, but the observer below saw it as normal. Such refinements need not concern the foil modeler; they are mentioned in order to point out how good design and proportion have developed over the centuries. Certainly, good proportion, and a sense of fitness of purpose in any design produced, should concern any designer.

USING GEOMETRIC DESIGNS

Geometric figures and solids constitute a sound basis for good design, and the beginner should become familiar with them. They may look difficult, but by carefully following each step of their construction they will be less so. Most of these figures are basic in design and, in fact, are rampant in nature in the cellular construction of plants, bees' honeycombs, seashells, and plant and flower forms.

Several good books are available on this subject, with macro-photographs to show the forms. Study them, and books on design, to see how these forms have been used in every age for decoration. Do not copy for your own use, but try to work out designs based on the many forms you encounter. You may combine geometric with natural forms, particularly when designing jewelry.

Figure 3. A Pre-Columbian hammered gold pendant disk, Veraguas style, from Panama.—Photograph courtesy of the Dumbarton Oaks Collection, Washington, D.C.

USING REPEAT DESIGNS

Another principle of design is the repeat. To understand this, draw a form, then place a small mirror on edge so that the form is reflected to form a repeat. A kaleidoscope, which has three mirrors mounted to give multiple reflections, can also be a helpful tool to a designer, converting common objects placed on a revolving base, into fantastic designs resembling jewels.

If repetition is combined with counterchange, as it is in some wallpaper and fabric designs, an overall pattern emerges which is not as might be supposed, monotonous, but rather it is harmonious. Designers make use of such techniques, and they should be borne in mind when creating a design.

Just as geometric forms may be combined to make a design, so may the solids—cubes, cylinders, pyramids, and others, especially when attempting sculpture with card or foil, or making ornaments for festive occasions.

DRAWING A DESIGN

Although drafting is a skill demanding much practice, learning how to make a working drawing is not difficult. Before attempting it, however, the student would be wise to study the subject to become familiar with the terms and rules for setting down a drawing. It is important to be accurate in measurements and their placement on a drawing. Even should the project be a simple rectangle with a design to be modeled, an accurate layout should be made and dimensioned, if only for easy reference at the time of cutting foil from a roll.

The drawing should also contain construction details. For modeling, this would be a note regarding which side to mark out the design, and which is first modeled. This is particularly important when using a foil with a different surface coating on each side. If the original drawing cannot be used to transfer a design to foil, make a tracing, or in some cases a pattern, for such use. Keep any patterns for future use, and file them with the drawings, as they may be used again.

In professional drafting, several different views of an object are made, so that a workman can understand what it should look like when completed. As many views are made as are necessary for understanding the shape of an object. This may mean a plan (top view), side and top and bottom elevations (views), plus oblique views to reveal hidden details not

Figure 4. Two hammered gold objects, Pre-Columbian. **Top:** *A gold pectoral of the Calima style from Colombia.* **Bottom:** *A pendant disk of the Veraguas style from Panama.*—*Photographs courtesy of the Dumbarton Oaks Collection, Washington, D.C.*

Figure 5. Cut-out object, possibly representing hummingbird moths. Made of hammered sheet gold, Paracas-Necropolis or early Nazca, from the south coast of Peru.—Photograph courtesy of the Dumbarton Oaks Collection, Washington, D.C.

seen in other views. In shop drawings it may never be necessary to make other than plan and side elevations, but if others are called for, it is essential to know how to make them. Be sure to place dimensions correctly, or they can be misleading.

If the chosen design is cylindrical, its circumference will need to be developed. Consider the label on a can to be that development in order to understand the principle. To lay out a drawing or pattern for a cone is more difficult, and if it is truncated (cut off at the top), even more so (see section on Development of Geometric Forms in chapter 3). Before cutting foil for such shapes it is advisable to first make a pattern from thin card stock in order to save both time and waste.

Chapter 2

BASICS OF FOILCRAFT

It is wiser to spend some time to learn what lies ahead in any craft than to plunge right in and meet with failure, thus dampening early enthusiasm. Success from the beginning with craft projects is important; therefore learn to know the tools to be used, and practice with them before attempting a serious project. It is equally important to get the feel of all materials to be used, and to know their inherent qualities and limitations.

There are several theories on ways to learn a given subject, some favoring courses from books, others individual instruction, and hardier souls believing that self-education is the best way. There is something to be said for all methods, but in the final analysis the person working at a craft nearly always has to find ways to learn by doing. Personal instruction being least likely, books and self-help must be the answer. Natural aptitude, sincere interest, and an ability to use tools are assets that cannot be disregarded, and which should be given serious thought before attempting a craft.

LEARNING TO USE THE TOOLS

The modeling of metal foils, unlike repoussé, is a comparatively easy craft to master. Relief designs can be produced by the use of wooden tools, whereas repoussé requires hammers and steel punches. The relief possible in foil, though somewhat shallower than repoussé, is adequate for most needs. Figure 4 shows that tools for modeling foil are few and simple, inexpensive to buy, or are readily made. Foils yield easily to gentle pressure, and will assume almost any form within reason.

How the tools are used is really a matter of logic. A broad, spoon-like tool will serve best for large areas that have to be modeled; the smaller tools—flat, wedge-shaped, and pointed—being used in restricted areas of a design. Experiment with each type of tool to see what can be accomplished with them.

BORROWING FROM OTHER CRAFTS

Techniques from other crafts are applicable as an aid to foil modeling, and it is advised that books on paper sculpture be consulted, especially in regard to the cutting and scoring methods which facilitate bending of the material, usually thin bristol board.

To become familiar with the scoring and folding of bristol board try the simple forms illustrated in figure 6, those on the right made from card, with duplicates in foil on the left. The latter were modeled freehand to show a need for an underlying form for this type of folding. Here is the first example of how cardboard forms can aid in shaping foil.

In drawings made for paper folding or sculpture, both solid and dotted lines are shown. This means that solid lines are scored on the face of the cardboard, the dotted lines on the reverse side. Scoring, which means lightly cutting the surface of the card, makes folding easier, and in the top right model in figure 6, it is easy to understand why scoring is done on both sides, because each section is bent in the opposite direction. Bear this in mind when making a drawing for a sculpture made of bristol board. Note also in the fourth example from the top the curves that can be made and folded. Such a technique is useful when forming parts of a sculpture, such as an animal head.

INGENUITY HELPS

Most crafts, in addition to the prescribed tools, have need for additional aids for shaping, bending, or otherwise manipulating the material. Foilwork is no exception. To understand this, look at the assorted shapes in figure 7, some possible time-saving devices for use when shaping raised borders, or making dimples or domes for ornamentation.

The lid from a food container has a built-in design that might be used on a piece of jewelry. The carved coaster would serve similarly. The long, straight pieces—half-round, V-section, and rope twist—can serve as forms for shaping foil. To do this the foil is positioned over the desired shape to conform to a design, and is first shaped with fingers and

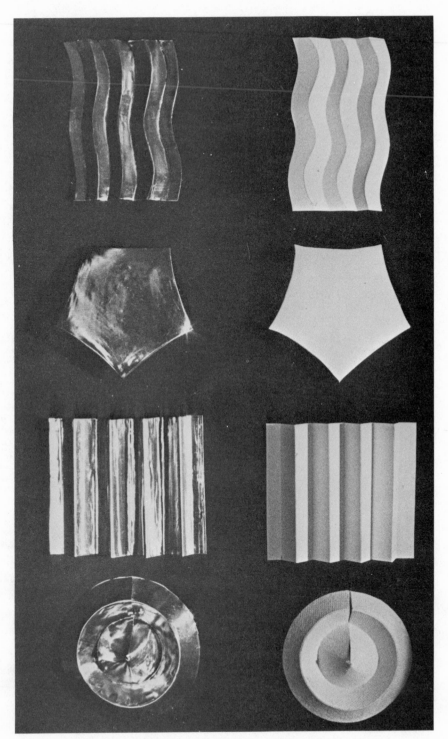

Figure 6. Sculptured forms in foil (left), and bristol board (right).

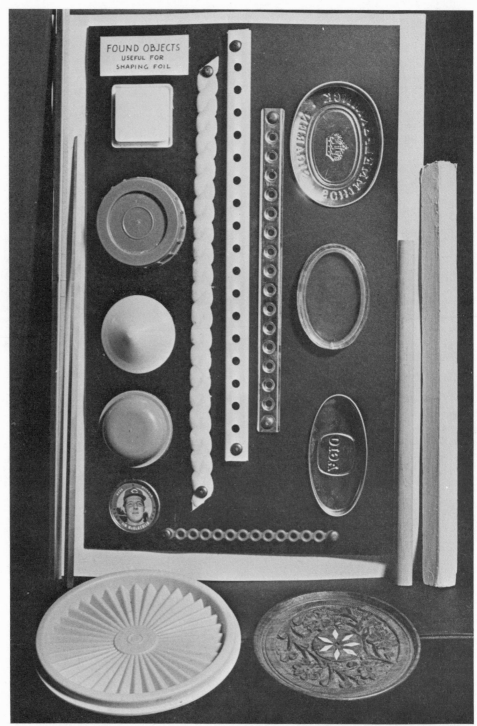

Figure 7. Everyday items useful in shaping foil.

thumbs, pinching the foil to conform with the underlying mold strip, after which a flat-sided tool is used to make a precise fit. If a corner is to be made, it is good to first make one up from the mold material. Figure 9 will help to clarify this technique. The strips with rows of holes will be found useful when there is a need to make dimples or domes in foil. To do this the form should be carefully positioned and fastened down in some way. The foil, previously marked to indicate the position of the domes, is laid over the mold. A domed tool is then used to press the foil into the depressions. Hand pressure may be sufficient, but a light tap on the end of the tool will give a sharper definition. A flat tool run along the foil over the mold will bring out the shape of the domes, but they may also need to have a pointed tool run around each one. Such forms may be made from plumber's strapping, a section of Meccano construction toy, or a handle from a shopping bag, such as the lower item in figure 7. It will be good to watch for and accumulate some of these aids, plus anything else with a surface texture that might be duplicated in foil.

SAMPLING THE CRAFT

Again, it is important to first get the feel of tools and the materials being worked with. Practice on small pieces of foil to see which tools are best for given situations. Trace a few designs on foil and practice cutting them out with scissors. It is not as easy as it might seem. Also practice with a knife to cut out parts of a design not accessible to scissors. These are the tools you will be working with most; so make sure you can use them before starting a serious project.

For practice, try the exercises shown in figure 8. Remember that borders can add rigidity to foil, so include them in your designs whenever possible. Texturing adds interest by contrast, and makes the surface of the foil less vulnerable to rough handling.

MODELING A STAR

In the star shown in figure 8 the scoring is on both sides, making it a fine example for practice as shown second from the top in figure 6.

First, construct a pentagon to produce the five points, then draw the outer lines to define the star. Connect all other lines to the center point, but remember to turn the foil over when transferring them for tooling. It is recommended that this star be made first of bristol board, in order to

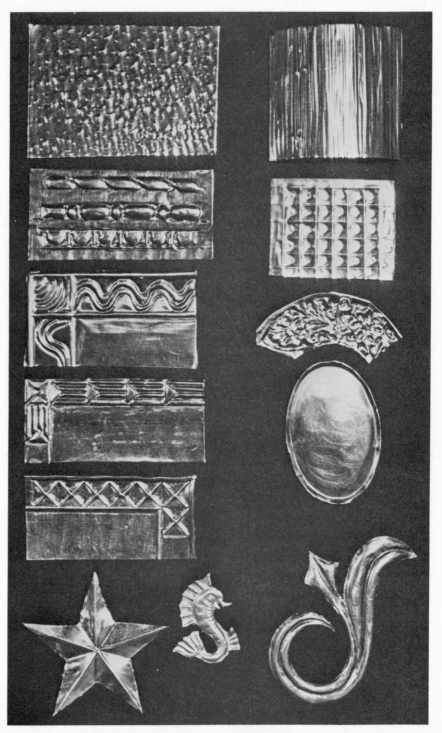

Figure 8. Some decorative motifs possible in metal foil.

gain practice in scoring before bending along the lines. It has already been pointed out to stress an important factor, always bend *away from* the scored lines.

For free-form modeling, draw a scroll or leaf form; both entail modeling from each side of the foil. Try to achieve crisp, decisive outlines and full modeling in such relief forms.

COVERING A PICTURE FRAME

We have touched on ways to shape foil over a form when making borders, which if practiced, should be sufficient preparation for covering a whole frame, using the same technique. Figure 9 shows how the foil is cut, and it is a wise precaution to first cut patterns from bristol board, after carefully measuring outside and inside dimensions of the frame. The miters are cut at an angle of 45 degrees, and should fit perfectly.

Check the corners of the foil to be sure the miters line up with those of the frame, which they will if the foil is cut correctly. Proceed with the shorter sides, covering them; then apply the long sides.

As may be seen from the drawing of a cross-section of the frame in figure 9, the foil is wrapped from the back of the molding to the underside of the rabbet (the groove in which the glass rests). Spread glue on the underside of the frame, and lay the cut foil on it. Turn the frame over and apply glue to the surface and sides. Bend the foil up and press into place with your fingers, running the forefinger along the edge to lay it flat. Bend it and shape it into the cove of the molding, smoothing it out along its length, and pushing the overhanging foil down and under. A flat modeling tool can now be used to sharpen the angles.

Should there be any overlap at the miters, cut through the foil at a 45-degree angle, and all will be well. This is one way to transform an old frame into a thing of beauty. Gold foil is quite handsome, as is silver.

COVERING A MOLDING IN REPEAT DESIGN

For a more ambitious project using the same technique, try making a modeled molding as illustrated in figure 9. Procedure is the same so far as measuring and cutting are concerned, except that the foil must be divided into equal sections for proper balance in the design. Lay this out first on tracing paper, transferring the design onto the foil.

After each piece has been modeled, decide whether the relief is such that it should be back-filled. Remember that pressure is applied to the foil

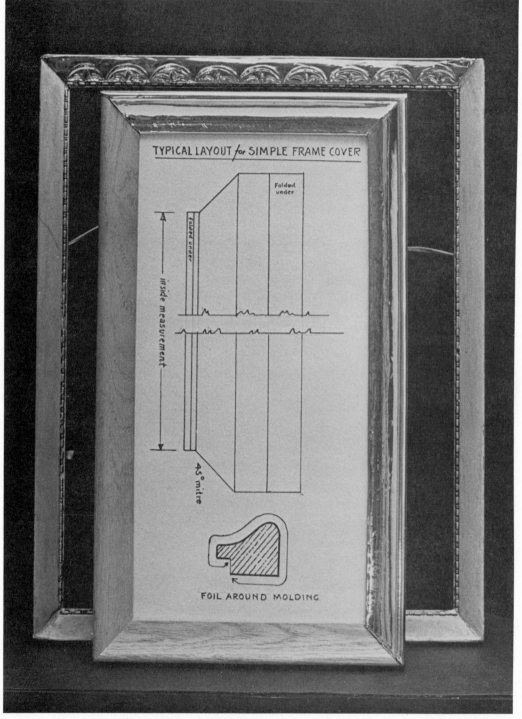

Figure 9. Modeled and plain foil as applied to a picture frame, along with simple how-to diagrams.

when gluing it to the frame. If such pressure is sufficient to dent the modeling, then it should be back-filled, but only the indentations will need this.

In the example shown, the surface of the frame is flat and slightly dished, meaning the foil will lie flat, not having to be shaped into a cove, as previously. Apply the modeled pieces with clear glue (Weldbond, or similar). To keep the foil in close contact, wind string along each side, just tight enough to maintain pressure. (The beaded edge shown in the frame in figure 9 was there when purchased, and is not modeled in foil.)

TRANSFORMING NOTHING INTO SOMETHING

Today almost everything we buy comes packaged, some items to an elaborate degree as in toiletries, with fancy bottles and sometimes fancier stoppers. Most of these are discarded but with foilcraft they might more profitably be recycled.

Just as an old frame may be given new beauty and usefulness, so might a humble can or plastic container be transformed by an application of foil, be it plain or modeled.

In figure 10 may be seen examples of common articles transformed with foils. A tobacco can becomes a humidor; a yogurt container a flower pot; and even one half of a perfume bottle carton is made to serve a useful purpose. A cardboard core for plastic tape becomes a napkin ring when covered inside and out with contrasting foils. Even the flower in the pot was modeled from foil, but has no sweetness to waste on desert air!

None of the pieces shown is difficult to make if care is taken in measuring and cutting the foil. The flower pot requires the knowledge of how to develop a truncated cone, because the foil can't just be wrapped around as in a container with parallel sides. (See section on Making Geometric Solids in chapter 3.)

MODELING A FISH

Demanding a greater degree of skill, the articles featured in figure 11 provide an opportunity for modeling a fish. A clear plastic detergent bottle is cut in half lengthwise, the cap end discarded, with the shape remaining suggesting that of a fish. Foil is modeled with scales, cut to conform to the plastic, to which it is then glued along the outer edges.

The fins, separately cut and modeled, are glued, one in a slot in the gill, the other to the top inside curve. The tail is unsupported by plastic. A

Figure 10. Foil-decorated everyday household objects.

domed eyeball is glued into a hole cut through foil and plastic. The fish suspends from a string tied to a wire loop secured to the back with plastic metal.

MODELING A LANTERN

The lantern details may be seen in a separate drawing, figure 12, in which the pattern for the conical top is laid out. The basis for this lantern consists of a frosted plastic bottle and tops from two sizes of aerosol spray cans. The cone is copper foil, soldered at the joint.

The candle shade, cut from a clear plastic bottle, is set in a discarded tire from a Tonka Toy, which has been sprayed a bronze color. The candleholder is a bottle cap (if the bottle's neck will not work as in the drawing), fixed to a lid from a plastic container. To decorate the dish (center) requires care in measuring, cutting, and applying the foil. Even though the construction materials prohibit burning the candle, the result is an attractive and decorative lantern.

MAKING JOINTS IN FOILCRAFT

There are times, as in the conical lantern top, when there is a need to make joints in foil articles. There are several ways to do this, similar to methods used in general metalwork in heavier gauges where joints may

Figure 11. Foil-decorated items designed using household discards.

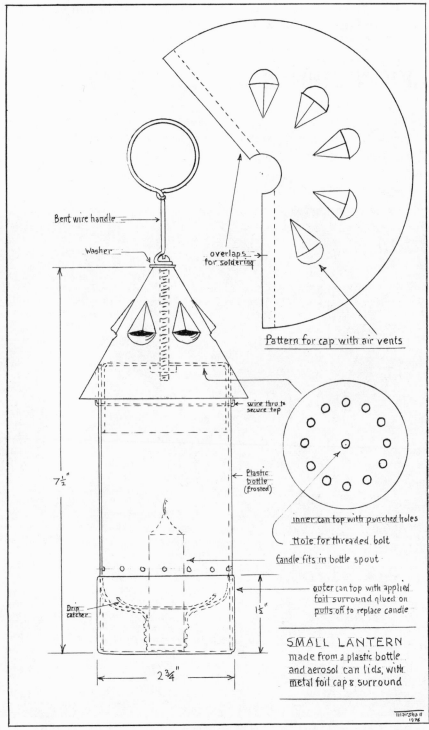

Bent wire handle

Washer

overlaps
for soldering

Pattern for cap with air vents

wire thru to
secure top

Plastic
bottle
(frosted)

$7\frac{1}{2}$"

inner can top with punched holes

Hole for threaded bolt

Candle fits in bottle spout

outer can top with applied
foil surround glued on
pulls off to replace candle

Drip
catcher

$1\frac{1}{2}$"

SMALL LANTERN
made from a plastic bottle
and aerosol can lids, with
metal foil cap & surround

$2\frac{3}{4}$"

marshall
1976

Figure 12.

be made by bending the metal over on the edges to be joined, then hammering them together into a tight fit. In foil, however, the edges are forced together with a flat tool.

For a tighter joint, it is better to solder the pieces together, and there are two ways to do this. The first is by heat from an electric soldering iron. Parts to be joined must be clean and free from grease. Each edge to be joined is first tinned; that is, solder is thinly applied.

Solders come plain or with a core of either resin or acid; the plain needs a flux to make it flow. Next, the two pieces are placed in contact and the soldering iron run along their length, causing the tinned portions to adhere. Any excess solder should be removed, because it blackens in time, disfiguring the object.

The second method of joining, known as "sweating," makes use of a gas torch in place of a soldering iron. The procedure is the same, but the joint must be held together by pressure when the torch is applied. The electric soldering iron method works well for foils of brass or copper. It is *possible* to solder aluminum, but more difficult, and needs special flux and solder. Epoxy resin glue serves very well to join this metal together.

USING AVAILABLE CRAFT SUPPLIES

In most craft supply stores are to be found many articles suitable for decorating with foils. These are the blanks produced for tole painters, who usually paint them with traditional designs. One such article is shown in figure 13, which when bought, was painted white. This object was chosen for the purpose of modeling a reflector to heighten the brightness of a burning candle. Just as in a lighthouse where the light is intensified by Fresnel lenses, so the light from the candle seems more intense when reflected from a modeled surface.

There is no great trick in making these reflectors requiring only careful layout and cutting, for even the modeling is simple, straight lines being made with a ruler. Two alternate designs are shown.

INSTANT "ANTIQUES" COPIED FROM MUSEUM PIECES

For those who would like to try duplicating the work of craftsmen of old, a visit to a museum featuring examples will prove useful, not only to

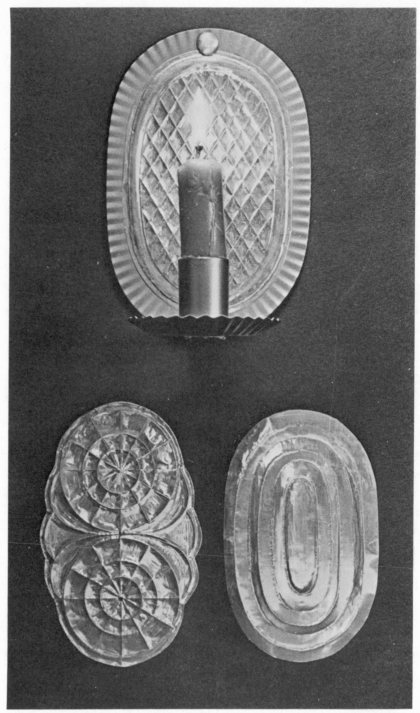

Figure 13. Modeled foil candle sconce with two alternate designs for the reflector.

see them at close range, but to obtain reproductions or photographs that might be found on sale there. The lower illustration in figure 14 was taken from a museum postcard, enlarged, then transferred to gold foil. The cutting was done before the piece was modeled, requiring great care with the scissors. The actual modeling was simple, but the effect is sophisticated when viewed in the proper light.

A greater challenge is afforded the foilcrafter who attempts a subject such as that at the top of figure 14. It is a copy of a gilded terra cotta relief from the island of Melos, in which Bellerophon, mounted on Pegasus, is shown slaying the Chimera. This is a pure modeling job, with no cutting necessary, the background being painted to give depth to the subject matter.

The frame, although machine made, was chosen for its ornamental border, which could as well have been modeled. Such subjects are appropriate for wall decorations, making a change from the ordinary. Their size is limited only by the width of foil available. Cleverly concealed joints might be considered for larger works.

HANDCRAFTING JEWELRY

One of the qualities of foil is its lightness, which makes it an ideal medium for jewelry. It is easy to stiffen by means of overall designs modeled into its surface, illustrated by figure 15 in the top three pieces. The fish at left have fins which convey a delightful sense of motion through water.

The fish, long a Christian religious symbol, is an appropriate motif for a cross. Note how the star in the top design is made by the meeting of the fishes, also true of the design at right. The overall modeling of the top three pieces makes them rigid and, although these were enameled with clear flux, this was done mainly to give a gold color to the copper from which they were made.

The two bottom pieces are not reinforced, but gain firmness through overall modeling. Note also the sense of motion in the design of each.

A square of enameled foil (fig. 15, center) is set into a wooden frame, and is backed by thin veneer. Provision is made for fitting a chain in order to use it as a necklace.

A note of caution when finishing jewelry projects: Leave no sharp or rough edges that might snag clothing or injure the wearer.

Figure 14. Two decorative pieces copied from museum exhibits.

Figure 15. Examples of modeled and enameled foil.

MAKING THREE-DIMENSIONAL FIGURES

A WEATHERVANE

An example of stiffening by overall design on a larger scale is shown in figure 16, a weathercock based on a 19th-century original, which as illustrated here, is single-sided. There is no reason why it cannot be made as a full figure by fitting two opposite sides together, with provision being made to solder them. The interior could be filled with plastic foam for lightness; ironwork would have to be made for interior bracing, and a pivot pin added which would sit in a socket. This is but one of many designs for weathervanes that were so common in ages past, but now are seldom seen except in folk museums, or in homes as wall decorations, for which the one shown here is intended.

Figure 16. Weathervane modeled in copper foil.

MAKING DECORATIVE MIRRORS

EAGLE-TOPPED FRAME

Figure 17, top, is a replica of a 19th-century girandole*, the basis for which was a brass-plated steel frame from a magnifying mirror, long since shattered and disposed of. The frame was split for the fitting of the original mirror and backing, allowing also for a replacement, which was secured by a tab fitted into a slot and bent over. To make this project clearer, a working drawing (fig. 18) has been made, which also shows the tools used to model the ornamentation.

The foil is cut and modeled in four separate pieces: the eagle, two side ornaments, and a bottom section. Each is shaped to conform to its respective area of the circumference of the frame. After modeling, the pieces are back-filled with plastic metal to strengthen them. In addition, braces are made from .040 gauge aluminum, and drilled to take wires for cross-bracing the modeled ornaments. When in place these wires are covered with plastic metal, which is smoothed neatly with a brush. The plastic metal is first thinned with acetone when applied in this way.

To enhance the rim of the mirror a frame may be made by cutting a disk of foil using a knife mounted in a beam compass. Before cutting out the center of the disk, a specially shaped tool, if mounted in the beam compass, will make a half-round molding after which the center is removed, leaving just the molded rim. The hollow half-round is filled with plastic metal before the rim is glued to the mirror with transparent glue (Weldbond or similar). Thus, a metal rim that might have been discarded may serve again in somewhat greater splendor!

MEXICAN-STYLED FRAME

The other mirror shown (fig. 17, bottom), will be a test of patience and cutting skill, but is proof that the repetition of a motif need not be monotonous. Made from silver aluminum foil, this mirror is reminiscent of old Mexican tinware.

A disk of foil is cut to the dimension desired, with the circumference of the mirror marked in. Draw an identical disk on paper, and divide the circumference into as many equal parts as the number of leaves desired.

---

*A girandole was originally a wall candelabra with mirror inserts but in the seventeenth century the term was used for mirrors minus candleholders.

Figure 17. Mirror frames of modeled foil.

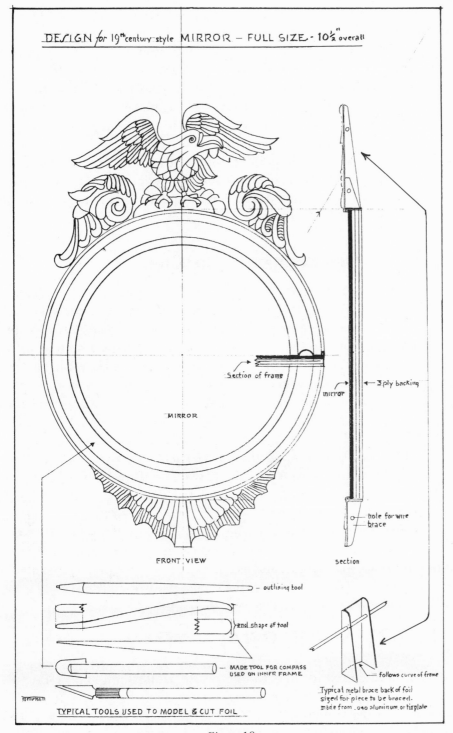

DESIGN for 19ᵗʰ century style MIRROR – FULL SIZE – 10½" overall

Section of frame

← 3 ply backing

mirror →

MIRROR

hole for wire brace

FRONT VIEW

section

– outlining tool

– end shape of tool

MADE TOOL FOR COMPASS USED ON INNER FRAME

follows curve of frame

Typical metal brace back of foil sized for piece to be braced. made from .040 aluminum or tinplate

TYPICAL TOOLS USED TO MODEL & CUT FOIL

Figure 18.

Draw in the leaves precisely, making provision for an outer line and center stem. With the right side of the foil turned up put a push-pin through the center to hold it in place; then position the drawing over it and tape it down. (If foil other than colored is used, either side may be utilized.) This should be done on a piece of board that can be turned as the design is being transferred. Faced corrugated board is good for this purpose, inasmuch as it is yielding enough to the tracing tool so that the design will be boldly transferred.

The leaf edges call for a pointed tool, as does the center vein, but the leaf itself will need a round-ended one, or wedge-shaped, rounded on the side used for modeling. Make each leaf match as closely as is possible, since variations will spoil the effect.

Plastic Hot-Melt Crystals as Backing

For the mirror project, clear plastic hot-melt crystals are used to give it added strength. First, lay a piece of kitchen foil over a cookie sheet, and in the center place an empty coffee can (or similar object). Lay the modeled circle which has in the meantime been cut to shape with scissors, on the can top, face down. Carefully place the plastic crystals (available from craft supply shops), on every leaf-back, heaping them up a little at the center; they will melt flat. Put into a 350-degree oven and close the door. In minutes the plastic will melt to a smooth surface.

Remove from the oven and see if there are any spaces remaining that need to be filled. If so, do this, then place back in the oven for remelting; this should be sufficient, and the mirror frame will have built-in stiffness.

Mount the mirror onto the disk with a few dabs of epoxy glue; weight down and allow to set.

A hanger may be affixed to the backing with epoxy glue or small screws. When hung, this mirror frame catches the lights in the room, adding sparkle to the decor, and as a project it will test patience, skill with scissors, and the ability to work with a repeat pattern.

MAKING A FOILCRAFT TRAY

An object intended for decorating by tole painters might be a tray, and this is featured in the next project, illustrated in figure 19. Instead of painting, it is decorated with foil, the center part being modeled. This particular tray has its sides covered with green aluminum foil, the center

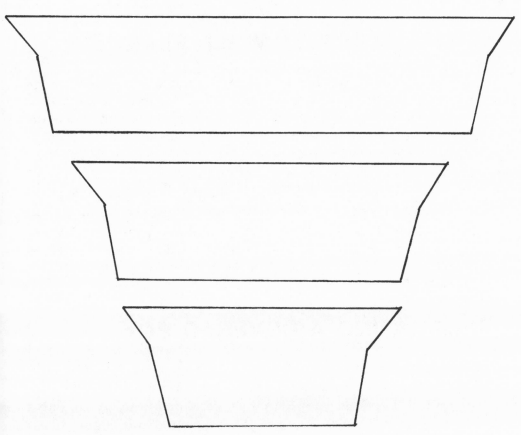

Figure 19. Metal eight-sided tray with modeled panel, and templates showing how to cut foil to cover the sides.

being gold for contrast. The patterns for the various sides are shown (fig. 19), and are angled in such a way that the corners fit perfectly. Provision is also made for the foil to be rolled over the wired edge of the tray and tucked up under it; any excess can be trimmed off with a sharp knife.

The sides are cut from foil and applied individually over a glued surface. The bottom piece is cut very slightly oversize to cover (when in place) the bottom edges of the side pieces. The design is traced onto the face of the bottom piece, after which it is turned over and modeled from the back. Final accenting is done from the face. For contrast, the background is textured by scribbling over it with a soft pencil, the marks from which are easily wiped off. This piece, if not used as a tray, can serve as a wall decoration if a hanger is soldered to the back before the foil is mounted. The patterns are shown full size, but the completed tray is photographed smaller.

MAKING A HORSE WALL PLAQUE

The horse plaque (frontispiece), scaled from a small picture of a weathervane, will present an opportunity to use the spoon tool shown in figure 2. This is ideal for modeling the large body areas, and most of the rest of the anatomy is done with various spoon-ended tools.

This horse is modeled on a sheet of foil 12 inches deep by 18 inches long, traced over a drawing enlarged by the squares method, as indicated by the small sketch. This piece took less time to model than some of the small jewelry. It is not cut out, but rather the background is painted blue to add depth to the horse. When finished it is backed with hardboard, and the edges of the foil turned over to the back. Two hangers are glued in place and it is ready to hang as a wall decoration.

DECORATING A COVERED BOX

Another object frequently used by tole painters is the whitewood box which comes in several sizes and shapes, each for a special use. We have chosen two different ones for the projects featured in figure 20, with a working drawing of one in figure 21. The box at the top of figure 20 has a recessed lid into which the modeled foil fits. Allowance is made in cutting the foil so that its edges can be turned down to form a shallow recep-

Foilcraft

56

Figure 20. Two wooden boxes decorated with applied modeled foil.

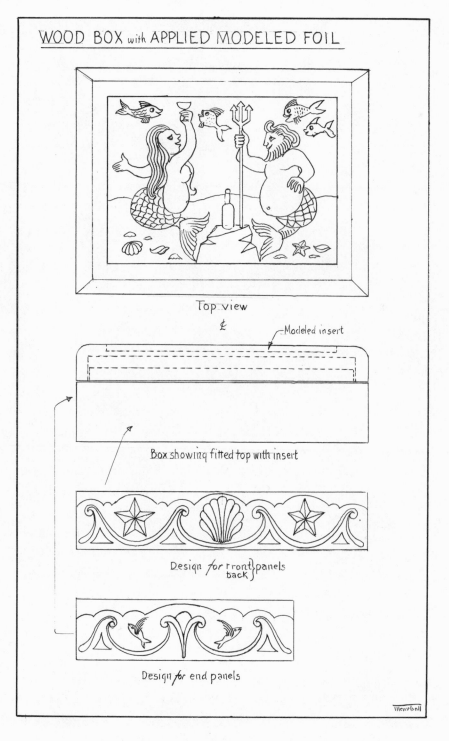

WOOD BOX with APPLIED MODELED FOIL

Top view
&

Modeled insert

Box showing fitted top with insert

Design for front panels
back

Design for end panels

Figure 21.

tacle making possible a thick layer of paste metal on the back to minimize denting of the ornament. The edges are beaded for added strength. Notice also that the background is recessed a little to produce highlights and shadows around the design.

If the sides of the box are covered with plain foil, one continuous piece may be cut to cover, requiring but one joint in the back. It is more convenient, however, to facilitate handling during modeling if each panel is cut separately.

After completion of the modeling of the side panels, they may be dipped in a bath of liver of sulphur (available at craft supply stores), which will produce a dark brown tone. After washing and drying, the pieces are rubbed with fine steel wool, highlighting the ornament in contrast with the background.

Back-fill the panels as described in the decorative mirror project. To mount the sections on the sides of the box, any good glue will serve, but the corners are best glued with epoxy cement to keep them from lifting.

The finished box is then given two coats of clear acrylic spray to prevent the inset metal from tarnishing.

RECIPE BOX

The recipe box (fig. 20, bottom) has only the top covered with modeled foil, which is finished in the same manner as the covered box (fig. 20, top). The ornamental border surrounding the name of the box is made up of sausages, a design imitative of the classic bead and reel. The body of the box is painted with bronze acrylic paint, produced by adding bronze powder to Liquitex Iridescent Bronze acrylic brush-on paint.

METHODS OF PRODUCING SIGNS USING FOIL

Metal foils have for many years been used in the sign industry, mostly for making the type of sign seen in various agencies or for the advertising of beer and liquors. These are made by the thousands, pressed in dies. Such signs are usually framed under glass to protect them. With this in mind look at figure 22 to get some idea of the possibilities of foil for making your own signs.

Figure 22. Sign and examples of lettering produced in modeled foil.

The inn sign at the top is typical of those used outside pubs in Britain, and on the continent of Europe. The original, from which this sign is copied, consists of an iron frame with the ornament in repoussé, and the applied letters filled with enamel—a very handsome sign indeed. The ornament is gilded, with the helmet silver for contrast. The frame is painted black and fitted with eyes for chains, which in turn hang from a wrought-iron bracket fixed to an oak post.

In the copy shown the ornament is made of silver aluminum foil surrounding the plaque of the Comet, an early locomotive design. The letters are painted with white acrylic paint, and the frame is black.

MAKING FOIL LETTERS IN RELIEF

Beneath the sign in figure 22 are examples of lettering modeled in foil. Several styles of letters are shown, modeled in half-round, and V-section raised and sunk. The cut-out letter is matt board covered with foil. The lettering is traced onto the foil face in all but the sunk V-section. This defines the outlines, and when the foil is turned over, the letters are easily modeled in relief.

Sometimes, especially when using copper or brass, the letters may need re-working from the front. If the depressions of the letters are back-filled, and the whole sign mounted on a stiff background, it will be strong and long-lasting.

The author once made a marker for a pet's grave, casting a slab of white cement into which was set a modeled plaque made from copper foil. It turned green with time, but remained otherwise intact, a testimony of durability. This sort of thing could put the gravestone-makers out of business!

MAKING CUTOUT FOIL LETTERS

In making cutout letters several materials may be used, such as matt board or hardboard. Because it is difficult to shape the foil around the curves of some letters, it is best to pick an alphabet style in which square forms are used. Cut out the letters, glue a rectangle of foil over each one; let the glue dry, then push with the forefinger over each one to reveal its shape. Having done this, make cuts with a sharp knife at all corners, then model the foil down over the edges, cutting away excess material. The sides need not be glued unless desired.

If a raised-letter plaque is required, the lettering may be cut from 6-ply bristol board and applied to a background of the same material lined for placement of the inscription. When the glue has set, a sheet of foil cut to size is placed over the laid-out lettering, and is fastened down with tape. With a finger rub over the whole inscription to reveal the letters, after which use a pointed tool to trace around them. The lettering will be raised just high enough so that curves will be no problem. When all stand out in relief, turn the plaque over and with paste metal thinned with acetone, paint the entire back. When dry, mount the foil onto a suitably stiff background.

If the foil is copper or brass it may be desirable to tone it as described in the process used on the covered box. Do this before painting on the filler. Rubbing with fine steel wool will accent the lettering and make it stand out from the background. A plaque so made will last for years if protected from abuse.

SAVE THOSE SCRAPS

After working with foils for any length of time many odd pieces of scrap will accumulate. Do not dispose of them, put them to use.

DESIGNING A MOBILE

One very good use of scraps is to make a mobile, one of those ever popular eye-catchers first introduced by the sculptor Calder, whose stabiles (similar to mobiles in construction, but stationary) are to be seen in museums and public squares around the world.

Almost anything can be dangled from strings to make a mobile, and things that float—such as boats, fish, and birds—seem very appropriate. Figure 23 uses fish that swim, and others that fly. In the latter the fins (wings) are modeled separately and fitted into slots, adding a touch of Duco glue to hold them firmly. The fish are hung from nylon fishing line, the mobile itself being mounted so that it may swivel. If located over a light, heat from the bulb will rise and put the fish in motion.

At Christmastime a mobile made up of ornaments and stars might add a festive air to a room.

Figure 23. A mobile utilizing scraps of foil.

DESIGNING A FOILCRAFT CLOCK

A decorative clock, though usually high in price, can be made inexpensively. The one shown in figure 24 has a 15-inch diameter dial, within which is a circle of textured foil with a twelve-pointed star superimposed. The movement is battery operated and costs about 15 dollars, available either at craft outlets or by mail order.

The clockface (dial) is cut from .040 gauge aluminum, obtainable in most hardware stores. It cuts easily with shears and has a polished surface that can be made matt by rubbing with fine steel wool.

Great care is needed to lay out and cut the twelve-pointed star. When cutting with a knife, always do so outside the line, with the ruler covering the design. Should the knife happen to slip, it will not damage the piece.

Place the cutout star, already glued on the back, onto the circle, keeping all the points equidistant from the outside edge. After the glue is

Figure 24. A clock dial with applied foil decoration.

thoroughly dry, place the disk on a textured surface, and with a round-ended tool rub until all the areas between the points of the star are textured. Glue the completed disk to the clockface. Again, keep the space around it equal, using a ruler or pair of dividers to check.

Draw the numerals on paper and transfer them to foil. Cut them out with scissors and knife, using a ruler for the straight lines, cutting the curves out freehand. In mounting these numerals it is wise to have a penciled outline of their positions marked on the dial. Use a minimum of glue, so that none squeezes out around the numerals, as any excess is hard to remove without marring the finish.

Cut out patterns for the hands from thin bristol board. Lay these on the foil and mark around them with a pencil. When cutting, allow ⅛ inch for folding over to stiffen the edges. Now, with Duco cement, affix the original hands to the backsides of those made from foil. When the glue has set, the hands are ready to mount. The movement is contained in a small case, having a central spindle onto which the hands are to be mounted. Drill a hole in the center of the dial to a size slightly larger than the spindle. This is best done before mounting the foil circle, which must also have a center hole (cut with a knife).

For hanging the clock, make a strip of .040 gauge aluminum long enough to bend over the top of the movement box and up. Make a hole in each end, one to go over the clock spindle, the other for hanging; place this over the spindle. Push the spindle through the hole in the face; fasten with the nut provided and tighten snugly. Push on the hands, the hour-hand first; then insert the battery, being careful to check its polarity, as marked plus or minus on the case, and the clock is completed.

JEWELRY FROM SCRAPS

After a sophisticated project, a change of pace might be welcome. Figure 25 offers some suggestions for jewelry with a chance to use up more scraps of foil. Work in this line offers an opportunity for original design. Even if designs of others are copied try to bring to them some innovation.

Rope-Skipping Fish

The top left example in figure 25 was cut from copper foil, with partitions modeled into the surface (champlevé) serving to keep the colored

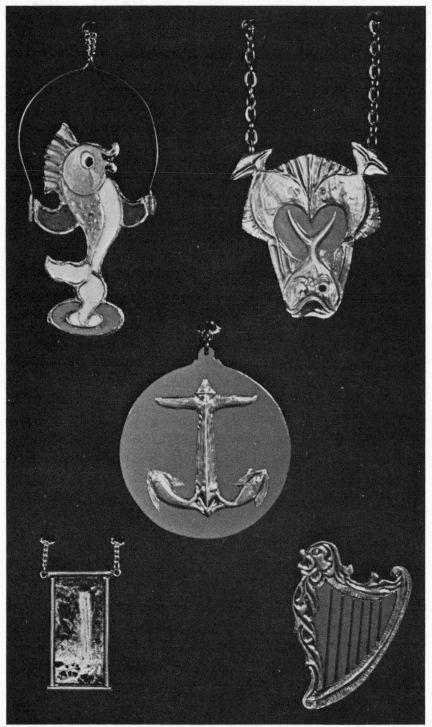

Figure 25. Foilcraft jewelry, some enameled.

enamels separate. The application of enamel stiffens the piece because it is applied to front and back. (For procedures and techniques, see chapter 8.)

The brass wire used for the skipping rope was soldered to the back of the fins after enameling.

Comedy and Tragedy Masks

Figure 25, top right, is an example of three fishes arranged to suggest the masks of comedy and tragedy, with the spaces defined as their mouths filled in with pseudo-enamel (a plastic powder available in several colors), that can be fired (melted) over a 100-watt light bulb, or in an oven set at 350 degrees. The pseudo-enamels are not as hard as true enamels, but they do serve to give color to a design.

Anchor

Figure 25, center, is in the shape of an anchor, made up of three fishes modeled in silver aluminum foil. This was back-filled then glued to a background of .040-gauge aluminum which was coated with pseudo-enamel to give contrast.

Mini-Art

A piece fired in true enamels (fig. 25, bottom left) is glued to a frame cut from silver aluminum foil. The sides of the frame are rolled on wire, the wires being left in to add rigidity. The top wire-ends are looped to take a chain.

Harp

The harp (fig. 25, bottom right) is modeled in silver aluminum foil and superimposed onto a previously prepared metal background, which is drilled to take the strings. The next step is to fire on the pseudo-enamel, after which the strings are set in place with a touch of Duco cement in each hole. The modeled piece is then glued to the background. A pin is glued onto the back, and—a finished brooch!

Figure 26. Foilcraft jewelry.

Figure 27. Foilcraft jewelry.

Figure 28. A pair of hammered gold earspools, Coclé style, Panama. These ornaments are Pre-Columbian, and are made in two sections so that one disk may be inserted from either side of the ear with one tube end fitting into the other.—Photograph courtesy of the Dumbarton Oaks Collection, Washington, D.C.

USING SMALLER SCRAPS

If there are still considerable amounts of scrap foil to work with, but the larger pieces are all used, think in terms of earrings or tie tacks. Figures 26 and 27 offer some suggestions along these lines, for which little information is needed. They take mostly all straight modeling; however, the term is lightly used, as some curves are in evidence.

In the octopus made of gold aluminum foil, two unlucky fish are caught in its tentacles. To contrast them with the octopus, the surface color is removed from the fish with acetone, exposing the silver beneath. A very fine, pointed brush is used for this purpose in order to avoid taking the finish off the tentacles. This touch adds unusual beauty to the piece. The eyes of the devilfish are painted red.

Chapter 3

MORE ADVANCED FOIL PROJECTS

A sound knowledge of the development of geometric solids is a prerequisite of the sheetmetal worker concerned with the construction of tanks, cylinders, ducting, and other forms. This same knowledge is useful to the craftworker in metal foils, although perhaps to a lesser degree.

Few working drawings can be made without some knowledge of geometric principles, and because many designs have geometric shapes, it is beneficial to know how to construct them.

MAKING GEOMETRIC SOLIDS

A beginner unfamiliar with geometric principles should not be discouraged. Figure 29 shows that when developed (laid flat), the figures are simple, yet when folded together they make decorative and sophisticated objects; several in combination are even more attractive. To gain familiarity with geometric forms, it is recommended that these be constructed of bristol board.

MAKING A HEXAHEDRON (CUBE)

The cube, a hexahedron, is a six-sided solid, simple to construct using thin (3-ply) bristol board as the material. All lines along which a bend will be made must be scored (lightly cut), with a round-ended knife (X-Acto), on the side of the board opposite the direction of the bend. The purpose of this scoring is to assure clean bends. Tabs are provided for the purpose of assembly, for which quick-setting cement (Duco) is used. It is a good

71

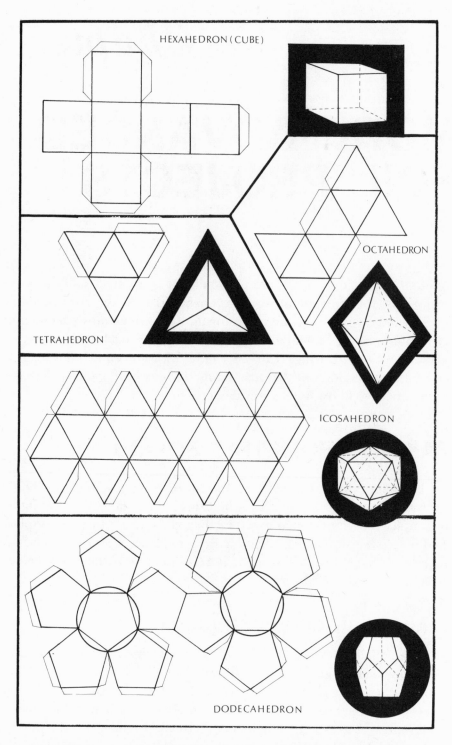

Figure 29. Development of geometric solids, showing the tabs necessary for assembly.

idea to snap rubber bands around the assembled solid until the cement sets up.

MAKING A TETRAHEDRON (PYRAMID) AND AN ICOSAHEDRON

After making the pyramid (a tetrahedron), it will be found that the other figures require only a little extra layout. The icosahedron may be a bit more difficult to assemble. In folding these multi-sided solids it is expedient to glue up and let set just half at a time, making sure the tabs are in contact. For the second half, bend the tabs less than 90 degrees, apply cement, then fold and put on the rubber bands. When tabs cannot be pressed into contact, this method of bending the tabs assures contact with the surfaces of the solid.

MAKING A DODECAHEDRON

Constructing a pentagon in a circle, basis for the dodecahedron, should present no difficulties; however, if it should, consult the section Construction of Geometric Forms, which appears a little later in this chapter. When scoring lines to be bent, disregard the circle (a necessary construction feature), and follow the folding procedure suggested for the icosahedron to secure the tabs.

It is much easier to construct these solids if they are made fairly large, although there may be times when smaller models are needed as in holiday decorations. If made from foil-covered bristol board, these solids are decorations in themselves.

The art of packaging today is highly developed, and much use is made of geometric solid forms, particularly in the cosmetics field. Some rather clever end closures are used, obviating the need for glues in packaging. Examples are shown in figure 30 for square, hexagonal, and cylindrical solids, along with construction details. They may look complicated, but the sections are consecutively folded one over the other, and if pushed inward remain in place. It should be obvious where to cut and where to score. Where dotted lines are shown, the bristol must be turned over for scoring along them, as they are to be bent in the opposite direction.

The geometric solids shown in figure 31 are quite handsome when made up with foil-covered bristol board. With care these can be made of

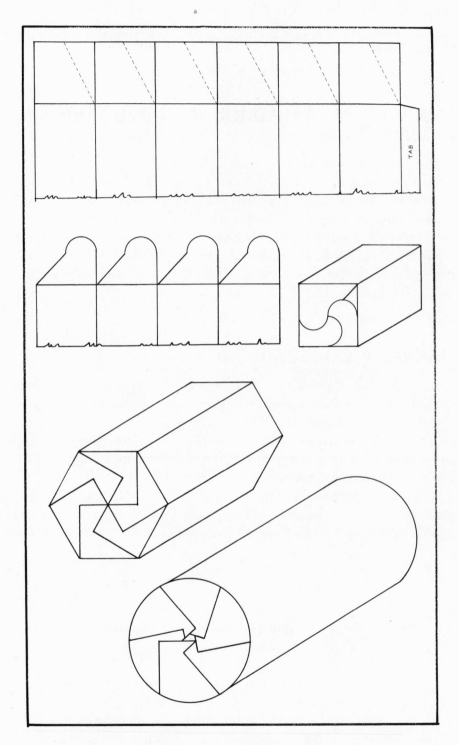

Figure 30. Layouts for end closures.

Figure 31. Models of geometric solids in foil over cardboard.

metal foil alone, but the bristol adds stiffness, and is easier to form without distortion.

To cut and fold the geometric solids is not much more difficult than laying them out, and it is always a pleasure to transform a drawing into an actual object. Figure 32 shows three examples of folded box ends plus three shapes made by folding and gluing, these being examples of how, by scoring and bending, some unusual forms can be made.

SIMPLER THAN IT APPEARS

Many people tend to shy away from anything that *looks* complicated, thinking the mechanics of construction beyond their capability. However, once the problems are tackled, they are found to be not difficult at all, merely demanding careful layout to achieve accuracy.

In some of the exercises, a certain amount of trial and error is called for to establish points, but no difficulty is encountered in so doing. Figure

33, numbers 1 and 2 are layouts for the two solids shown to the left and to the right in figure 32.

CONSTRUCTION OF GEOMETRIC FORMS

Figure 33, Number 1. The hexagon, a six-sided figure, is constructed by stepping off around a circle its own radius, which is six times. By joining these points a hexagon is formed. From three alternate points of the figure draw lines as shown, meeting at the center of the circle.

By trial and error locate centers on these lines from which to strike radii to form arcs that intersect at three points. To form the solid, cut out the circle and score all lines from one side. The arcs on each side of the hexagon form the tabs for gluing the solid together. By pinching along the curves the solid takes shape (fig. 32, center and right). Shapes like this, or modifications thereof, will prove useful when making foil sculptures.

Figure 32. End closures and modeled forms in bristol board.

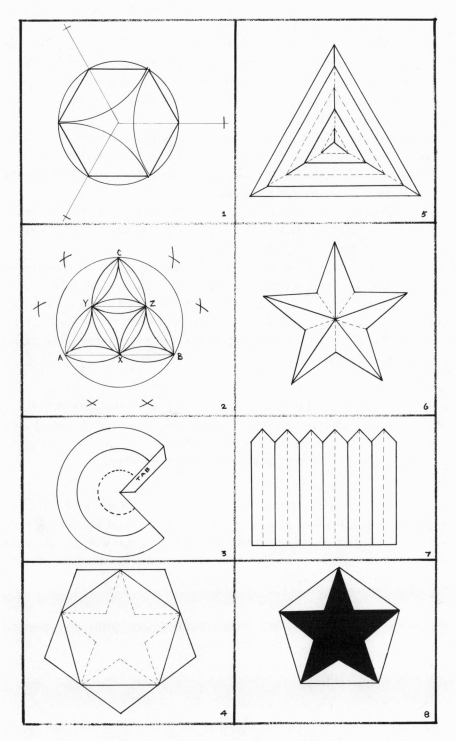

Figure 33. Construction methods for folded forms.

Figure 33, Number 2. The left-hand solid in figure 32 is shown developed in figure 33, number 2, and is based on the triangle, in which are four smaller triangles on all sides of which arcs are inscribed. Draw a circle and inscribe within it triangle ABC by setting off three points around its circumference (using the radius of the circle). Join the three points to form the triangle.

Form the four small triangles within the larger triangle using AX as radius to strike points X, Y, and Z. Join the lines as shown. Using the same radius, strike arcs from A, B, and C and X, Y, and Z to produce centers for inscribing arcs on the small triangles.

After making the six inner arcs in this manner, strike the outer arcs from X, Y, and Z. The trick is in maintaining the same radius as of the point where AX has been established.

To form the solid, cut out the large triangle along the arcs; then score all lines except the straight construction lines, and form the solid, half at a time. Remember the trick taught in the forming of earlier solids, and bend the tabs at less than 90 degrees, so that they make good contact when folded in. This neat little solid makes a nice ornament, especially if in foil-covered bristol board.

Figure 33, Number 3. This is the drawing for the wheel shown in figure 6, where it is made up in both bristol and foil. Note that the small inner circle is scored from the side opposite to the central one. This shape is a light-catching ornament when suspended from its edge.

Figure 33, Numbers 4 and 8. The finished version of number 4, number 8 is a pentagon folded over to reveal a star. If colored aluminum foil is used to make this ornament, the bent-over parts will be silver for contrast. This makes a good Christmas ornament. Incidentally, the Chrysler Company logo is formed in this manner.

Figure 33, Number 5. A three-dimensional figure, number 5 requires scoring from both sides. The small inner triangle is poked up with a pointed tool. If this is first made up in bristol board, it can serve as a mold over which to model foil.

Figure 33, Number 6. After scoring from both sides, the star can be pinched into shape with the fingers.

Figure 33, Number 7. The fan fold must be scored on both sides. In order to form a fan it is first pinched together, then spread in the fan shape while pinching at its base.

DEVELOPMENT OF GEOMETRIC FORMS (As shown in figure 34)

In figure 34 are shown developments you will need to know if a project calls for a conical shape. A lampshade, for instance, is a truncated cone; that is, one that is cut level with the base. If cut at an angle, the top curve must be plotted to produce the oval formed when joined. As may be seen, development means laying flat a given shape. A label taken from a can is a development of a cylinder (if the can is round).

Truncated cone. To develop a truncated cone, a drawing is made with a side elevation and a plan of its base. Lines are continued up the sides to the apex of the cone, which is then the center from which arcs are drawn from the top and bottom of the truncated cone. The plan of the base is divided into a convenient number of points around the circumference, which are then stepped off along the struck bottom arc. Lines are then drawn from these points to the apex of the cone. Allow an extra space for overlap, and the pattern is ready for cutting out and folding into shape.

Angled, truncated cone. The development for a cone truncated at an angle is essentially the same as described above, except that the oval top is plotted by first drawing lines parallel to the base line as shown, then with dividers stepping the distances off from the outside lines of the stretch-out in both directions toward the center. A line drawn through these points will produce the curve that forms the top of the truncated cone. This shape is not likely to be needed except when making a sculpture.

The bottom example, an intersection, is shown to demonstrate the plotting necessary for what looks like a simple right-angle joint of two pipes.

SUGGESTIONS HELPFUL IN DESIGN LAYOUT

Number 1, figure 35, shows a method of dividing a line into a given number of even spaces. Draw a line at any angle and length from A, and

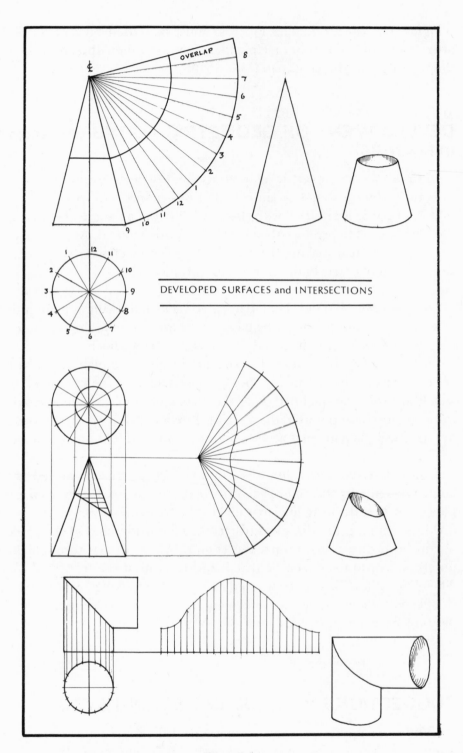

DEVELOPED SURFACES and INTERSECTIONS

Figure 34.

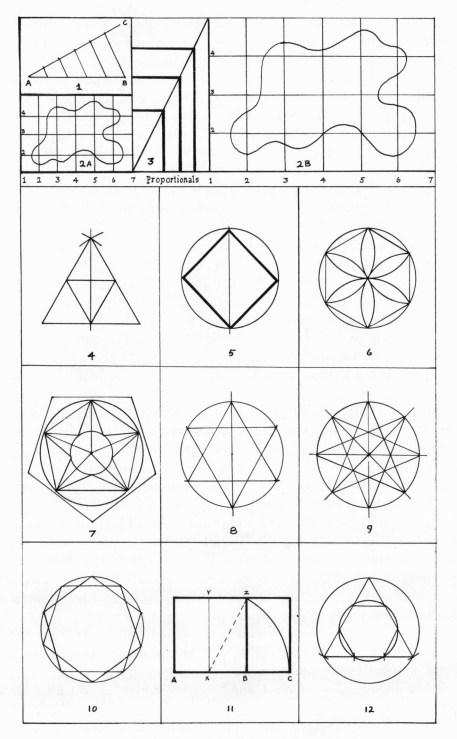

Figure 35. Helpful construction details for working drawings.

with a ruler or dividers step off the number of spaces desired. Draw a line from B to the last point on AC; then draw lines from the other points parallel to it. AB will then be divided into equal parts.

Numbers 2A and 2B, figure 35, show a method of enlarging a drawing by the proportionate squares method. Draw a grid of squares over the drawing, say 1 inch in size; then, having determined the degree of enlargement desired, draw squares in direct proportion, perhaps twice as large (2 inches). Number these on both drawings to help locate areas to be filled.

Copy the lines of the smaller drawing onto the squares on the larger sheet. Although only approximate, it is surprising how accurately a drawing can be copied in this manner.

To reduce a drawing, reverse the process.

Number 3, figure 35, shows enlargement of rectangles by the diagonal method. Lay the rectangle to be enlarged onto a sheet of paper of a size to accommodate the anticipated new size. Draw a diagonal line from its bottom left corner through the top right angle to a length needed for the new rectangle. Measure along the bottom line the size required, and from it erect a perpendicular line to meet the diagonal. Project a line from this point parallel with the base line, and the desired rectangle will be formed.

Number 11, figure 35, shows what the ancient Greeks deemed to be the perfect rectangle, which came to be known as the golden mean. It figured in much of their architecture, and that of succeeding ages. Jay Hambridge in his book, *Dynamic Symmetry,* has much to say on this heritage from the Greeks, and Maitland Graves in his book, *The Art of Color and Design,* also deals with the subject in some detail.

To construct this paragon of proportion draw a square and divide it in half. With X as the center and XZ as radius, strike an arc. Continue AB to C and erect a perpendicular from it. Project a line from Z parallel with AC to meet it, and the perfect rectangle is formed. Unity is created by repetition of the golden mean ratio, 1:1.618, which was used by the artist da Vinci in his *Annunciation* painting. Seurat, the French impressionist painter, was another who scaled his paintings to this formula.

It is interesting to note also that the art of the ancient Arabs, who were great mathematicians, makes much use of geometric figures. The term *arabesque* denotes a style which combines geometric forms with natural forms.

The remaining diagrams in figure 35 show how various geometric figures may be combined to make designs. Their construction is self-evident, requiring only careful measurement or stepping off with dividers. Several kinds of stars are made possible by combining triangles and pentagons.

A knowledge of the design and making of geometric solids is not just a useless exercise; in fact, this knowledge will prove most useful when planning to make sculptures of foil or foil-covered bristol board.

AIDS TO GEOMETRIC CONSTRUCTION

Almost every craftsperson will at some time be required to construct as a basis for a design a geometric figure, and for those who don't know how or those who need a refresher lesson, construction methods are described. Once mastered and made use of, these figures become second nature to construct. For anyone who makes constant use of them, it is a good idea and a time-saver to make up master patterns of each, possibly a 6-inch size, from which duplicates and larger or smaller adaptations can be made. Master patterns may be made from matt board or thin metal.

Another way is to make a master drawing of each from which photostats can be made to any size required. Such copies are inexpensive, but again there may be a delay getting to the store and back. If this method is used, it would be wise to get several sizes done at one time, the negatives then being filed for future use.

Drafting supply stores often carry plastic sheets on which the more common geometric figures are stamped out, and from these sheets they may be traced. Some school drawing sets also feature the same idea. However, it is often quicker to construct the figure to the size required, using the procedures here outlined.

CONSTRUCTION METHODS

Regular polygons. There are general and specific methods of constructing these polygons. The general method, as in figure 36, numbers 1, 2, 7, 8, and 9, applies equally to all polygons, but in particular polygons the special method is sometimes shorter and more accurate, as in 3, 4, 5, 10, 11, and 12. Remember the following important facts concerning regular polygons:

•Lines that bisect the angles of regular polygons meet in one point,

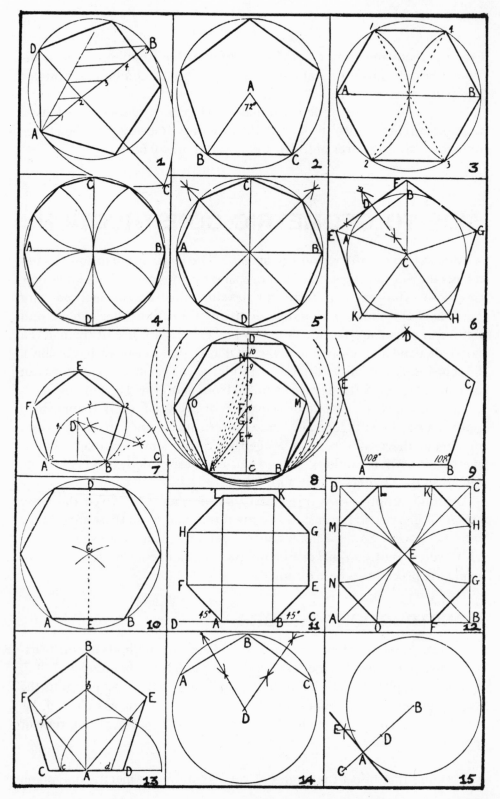

Figure 36. Aids to construction of geometric forms.

which is the center of the figure, and they divide the polygon into a number of equal triangles (Figure 36, numbers 5 and 6). In the hexagon these are isosceles.

•The center of the polygon is the same as that of the circle to which the sides of the polygon are tangent (the *inscribed* circle) and also the *circumscribed* circle which passes through the angular points (see numbers 1 through 8).

•The sum of all the interior angles is equal to twice as many right angles as the figure has sides. This affords a ready method of constructing any regular polygon by means of the protractor, as in number 9 when the side is given—a fact made use of in surveying.

Construction Methods Demonstrated (figure 36)

Number 1. In a given circle to inscribe any regular polygon (approximate method). Draw the diameter AB and divide it into the same number of equal parts as the figure has sides (say 5). With A and B as centers and AB as radius, make arcs intersecting at C. From C draw CD, always through the *second* division on AB, cutting the circle in D. Join AD, which is one side of the pentagon required. Set off AD around the circle and join points as shown.

Number 2 (another method). Draw any radius AB. At the center A make an angle with AB equal to 360° divided by the number of sides of the regular polygon required (say a pentagon). Thus 360° divided by 5 = 72°. Therefore, make the angle BAC = 72°. Join BC, which is one side of the pentagon. Set off BC around the circle, and join the points as shown.

Number 3. To inscribe a regular hexagon in a given circle (special method). Draw any diameter AB. With centers A and B, and radius equal to that of the circle, cut the circle in 1, 2, 3 and 4. Join the points as shown.

Number 4. To inscribe a regular duodecadon in a given circle (special method). Draw two diameters AB and CD perpendicular to each other. With centers A, B, C, and D, and radius equal to that of the circle, describe arcs cutting the circumference of the circle. Join the twelve points as shown.

Number 5. To inscribe a regular octagon in a given circle (special method). Draw two diameters AB and CD, as in number 4. Bisect each quadrant thus formed, cutting the circumference as shown. Join the eight points.

Number 6. To describe any regular polygon about a given circle (general method). Divide the circumference into as many equal parts as the figure is to have sides (say 5 for a pentagon). From the center C draw lines through each point. Draw AB, one of the sides of the inscribed pentagon. Bisect AB by the perpendicular CD, cutting the circumference in D. Through D draw the tangent EF parallel to AB, cutting CE in E, and CF in F. Make CG, CH, and CK each equal to CE or CF. Join F, G, H, K, and E as shown.

Number 7. On a given line AB to construct any regular polygon (general method). Produce AB, and with center B and radius BA describe a semicircle, and divide it into the same number of equal parts as the figure has sides (say 5). Join B with 2. Bisect AB and B2 by lines intersecting at D. With D as center and radius DA or DB, or D2, describe a circle. Set off AF and FE each equal to AB. Join the points thus obtained.

Note: In this construction great care is required in dividing the semicircle correctly, which may be done with the protractor. As there are 180° in a semicircle, divide 180° by the number of sides the polygon will have; thus 180° divided by 5 = 36°. Then make the angle CB1 equal to 36°, and mark off C1 around the semicircle as shown. The semicircle may be divided into *four* equal parts with the 45° triangle (as used by draftsmen), and into *three* equal parts with the 60° triangle.

Number 8. Another general method. Bisect AB by the perpendicular CD. Make CE equal to AC or BC. With center B and radius BA describe an arc cutting CD in E. E and F are respectively the centers of circles belonging to the square and the hexagon. Bisect EF in G. With center G and GA or GB as radius, describe a circle, and set off AB around it. Join the points, and ABMNO is the pentagon required. By making 6-7, 7-8, 8-9, etc., each equal to 4-5 or 5-6, we obtain centers for the heptagon, octagon, etc., as shown.

Number 9. Another general method using the protractor. The number of degrees in each angle of a regular polygon may be found as follows: From twice as many right angles as the figure has sides, subtract four right angles, and divide the remainder by the number of angles in the figure. Suppose a regular pentagon be required. As it has five sides, from *ten* right angles deduct four, and the remainder is six right angles. Then (90° × 6) divided by 5 equals 108°. At A and B make angles of 108°. Make AE and BC each equal to AB. With E and C as centers and AB as radius make arcs intersecting at D. Join the points as shown.

For a nonagon the angle would be found thus: From eighteen right angles deduct four, leaving fourteen right angles. Then (90° × 14) divided by 9 = 1260° divided by 9 = 140°.

Number 10. To describe a circle around a regular polygon. With AB as radius and A and B as radii strike arcs cutting each other at C on the perpendicular ED. With C as center and CA as radius, describe a circle which will touch all points of the hexagon.

Number 11. To construct an octagon of any desired size. On a baseline DC erect perpendiculars at A and B, AB being one side of the octagon desired. With a 45° triangle draw lines from A and B. With radius AB and centers A and B strike arcs to give points E and F, through which draw a line parallel to AB. Make the center square continuing the lines as shown. Erect perpendiculars from E and F to G and H. GK and HL are drawn at 45° angles. Complete the figure as shown.

Number 12. To inscribe an octagon in a given square ABCD. Draw the diagonals AC and BD. With centers A, B, C, and D, and radius AE (half the diagonal), describe arcs cutting the sides of the square in F, G, H, K, L, M, N, and O. Join FG, HK, LM, and NO. Then FGHKLMNO is the required octagon.

Number 13. To construct any regular polygon, having the diameter AB given. Through A draw CD perpendicular to AB. Take any convenient distance Ac, and make Ad equal to it. Upon cd construct, say, a regular pentagon cdebf. From A draw lines through e and f. From B draw BE and BF respectively, parallel to be and bf. From E and F draw ED and FC parallel to ed and fc. Then CDEBF is the required pentagon. It should be noted that the diameter divides the polygon into two equal parts. In a polygon with an *equal* number of sides, the diameter passes through the center, and is terminated at the middle points of two opposite and parallel sides, as DE in number 10; but in a polygon with an *odd* number of sides, it passes through the center from one angle to the middle point of the opposite side, as AB in number 13.

Number 14. To describe a circle passing through three given points, A, B, and C. Join AB and BC. Bisect each by the perpendiculars intersecting at D. With D as center, and DA or DB or DC as radius, describe the circle required. This problem shows how the center of a circle may be found by assuming any three points in its circumference, how to describe a circle about a given triangle, and how to describe an arc equal to a given arc with the same radius.

Number 15. To draw a tangent to a circle through a given point, A, in its circumference. Find the center B, draw the radius BA, and produce it to C. Make AC equal to AD (any convenient distance). With centers C and D, and any radius, describe arcs intersecting at E. Draw AE, the required tangent.

These are just a few of the many geometric problems to be dealt with in constructing foil projects. It may be wise to have on hand a complete book for reference (see Bibliography).

Although it is possible through trial and error to construct certain shapes, it is more practical to learn how to do the job properly, thus saving both time and possible waste of material. Much layout work demands just common sense and a little forethought.

Chapter 4

FUNDAMENTALS OF FOIL SCULPTURE

Figure 37 illustrates how the various geometric solids can be combined and given new meaning as part of a sculpture.

PRELIMINARY STEPS

Before rushing to cut and fold foil to make a sculpture it is wiser to first make some sketches of the proposed project, followed by a working drawing and the development of each component.

It is best to do a first model using bristol board, which can later serve as a template in laying out the foil. There may be a need for some cutting and fitting where parts come together, although it should be possible to work these joints out on paper, using geometric means.

For greater rigidity combine the cardboard and foil when constructing the sculpture.

Choice of foil is important in making sculpture. Copper and brass are not only stiffer, but may also be soldered, an important consideration in assembly. Aluminum foil is softer, and must be assembled with glue or cement, which sometimes presents a problem of how to clamp parts together until the glue sets up. Such assembly problems should be studied at the design stage, and when making the working drawing.

The ingenuity of the foilcrafter will often be challenged in deciding just how to hold parts in place when glued. A stout armature may be the answer if strong support is called for.

The method of fastening parts of a sculpture together is important, as is also the knowledge of how to solder when necessary, and knowing the

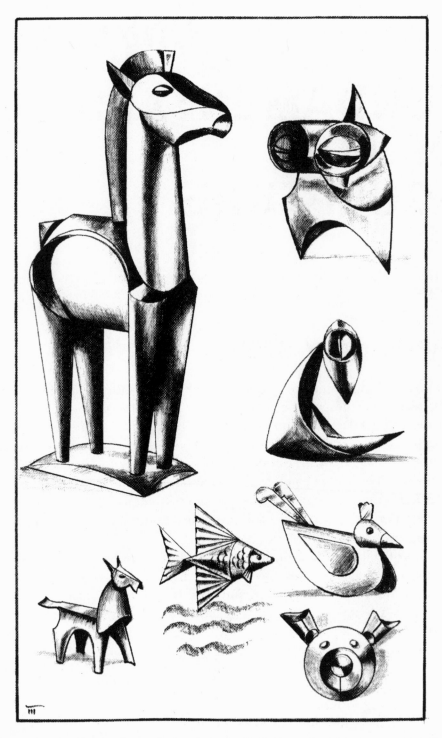

Figure 37. Sketches of sculptures that can be made of foil. The top three figures were made by Peggy Specht for the NVF Company of Wilmington, Delaware.

Figure 38. Sketch for a sculpture in metal foils.

glue or cement best for any given purpose. A quick-setting cement such as Duco is useful for assembly of solids, but a so-called universal bonding adhesive like Weldbond is usually the better choice for permanent assembly.

The advertised "miracle" glues (for example, Eastman 910 Adhesive, DURO Adhesive, and Krazy Glue) are to be avoided, as not only are they expensive, but also tricky to use, particularly in inaccessible places.

KEEPING IT SIMPLE

Although the construction of a sculpture may be an exciting project, there are other three-dimensional forms that may be better for a beginner. A vase made from two truncated cones is not difficult to make, and if of dissimilar metals—brass and copper—may not only be soldered together, but may also be finished in contrasting tones for interest. An oversize flower with foliage might then be made and used in the vase.

The model-maker does not call his work sculpture, even though it is usually three-dimensional. A model locomotive constructed from strong cardboard and covered with foil makes a handsome decoration, one to delight any small boy—or his father, for that matter. An Erector set has components useful for the framework, which can be assembled with small nuts and bolts. Figure 39 is an example, parts of which came from plastic containers. The wheels are cut out like cookies from plastic clay that when oven-baked becomes hard.

Metal foil is also ideal for coppering the underside of a model ship, and may be left natural or antiqued green by chemical action.

Making A Sculptured Mobile

For a beginner perhaps the easiest sculpture may be in the form of a mobile, now an object known to many children from their earliest days. Mobiles are excellent ways to make use of scrap pieces of foil, by transforming them into forms that fly or swim, either flat or in the round. An example is seen in figure 37 in which the fish is constructed of two cones joined at the center, with added fins and tail. This can be made with a complete cone for the forward part, and two half-cones incorporating the fins forming the rear section. The tail can be fitted into a slot at the apex of the cone.

Figure 39. Model railroad engine made of foil and household discards.

As may be seen, the pig's head (bottom right, fig. 37), is made from a series of truncated cones, the nose of the smallest one being capped. The ears are provided with extra tabs, which are glued to the inside of the cone forming the head. This small sculpture is a practical application of the geometric solids, thus proving that they are rewarding to make when used creatively.

The horse (bottom left, fig. 37), is a simple but effective way to make a small foil sculpture, requiring only a flat piece of foil cut to shape and folded over, allowance being made when cutting the foil to shape the partial cones forming the legs. The head and neck are separately formed, with provisions made for fastening them together.

The top three sculptures (fig. 37) were made by Peggy Specht for the NVF Company of Delaware, to promote the use of their product, Forbon, in making paper sculpture. These projects are readily adapted to foil.

HOUSEHOLD FOILS BACKED WITH BRISTOL BOARD

In addition to the metal foils already described, there are other materials, such as household foils and foil papers that can be used for a variety of projects, but particularly for sculpture.

To prepare materials, plenty of space is needed on a bench or table top, along with quantities of old newspapers. It is a good idea to make up a supply of foil-coated bristol board for future use, because the process is rather messy. Lay a sheet of bristol board on a smooth board and surround it with newspapers to catch the overspray. Apply the adhesive. (The easiest to use are the aerosol types, one of which is Scotch Sprament.) It is recommended that the spray be laid in two directions to assure an even coating.

Onto the sprayed surface carefully lay household foil, regular or extra strong, and with a roller or squeegee, smooth it down, being careful to avoid bubbles or creases. Lay the sheet aside under a piece of hardboard to keep it flat.

Proceed to do the same with other sheets of bristol and foil (or foil paper), replacing the newspaper after each spraying, and being careful to keep the spray off surrounding articles. (Some overspray is unavoidable.)

In place of spray cement one of the so-called universal glues may be used but be sure to read the label as not all glues are suitable for use on metallic surfaces. If glues other than the spray type are used they should be evenly brushed over the surface of the bristol board so that when rolled, the foil will be flat.

When applying household foil, take the roll from its box, and after carefully laying it onto the glued surface, roll out enough to cover the whole board; then cut it off. If rolled with care it should be smooth as if rolled with a roller. While performing this task it is advisable to use several types of foil, from the type used for modeling to household foils and foil papers. With a supply on hand, experiments can be conducted to find the best uses for each type.

Test several types of adhesive too, and make notes on which serves best for each purpose. Avoid the so-called contact cements; they are too hard to handle unless two people work together in positioning the foil. Bubbles or creases that occur at times cannot be eliminated if contact cement is used.

FOIL ON SELF-STICKING VINYLS

Experiment with the various types of self-sticking vinyls available. These come with a backing paper to protect the adhesive with which they are coated. Foils can be applied to the face of these vinyls with any of the glues just mentioned; then just follow directions for applying, which are printed on the backing paper.

Certain of the self-sticking vinyls come transparent with an overall pattern printed on them, and are used to "frost" windowpanes, or to add pattern over other plain surfaces. These vinyls can be applied over foil to give an added dimension.

From all this it is apparent that the worker in foils has quite a selection of materials with which to work. Foil papers, which come in several colors, may be mounted on any suitable backing, using the paste prepared for applying vinyl wallpapers.

Part II

ADVANCED METALCRAFT

AN INTRODUCTION TO ADVANCED METALCRAFT

Foilcraft is a fascinating art form and can be enjoyed in its simplest form, using household discards and tools gathered from the kitchen; or it may be that foil sculpture utilizing geometric forms is favored—a rather complex and interesting craft. Whether the project might be that of making a mobile, making jewelry, enameling on copper, or conjuring up "museum pieces" to decorate the home, most of the projects in Part I were relatively simple. If metalworking in more advanced methods sounds interesting, there are many crafts to be explored in Part II.

Foilcraft itself may be made more interesting by learning the ways of making molds and dies in order to mass-produce jewelry, trays, dishes, plaques, or club emblems—perhaps for a bazaar, or gifts for family and friends, or even as a profitable business.

Using foil in the round; spinning metal on a lathe to form bowls, plates, and trays; or making holiday decorations—all lead the craftsperson onward until new horizons are found. Repoussé, high relief in heavier metal, might well be the next progression, or perhaps enameling on copper is of interest; if so, cloisonné and champlevé are dealt with, explaining the differences and outlining the methods.

Formulas for advanced metalworkers are given to achieve various finishes on different metals. Formulas for etching are also included.

Some insights into nearly every type of metalcraft are given, including the casting of lead statuary. Gilding, from its history to its application, is another satisfying craft adjunct.

If an object can be imagined as being made of metal, there is a method outlined that can be followed in order to produce it.

Chapter 5

DUPLICATING FOIL COMPONENTS

It quite often happens that a particular project has repeat motifs that would be tedious to make individually. Such components may be made by any of several methods, and while hand-modeling is still called for, the process is easier and quicker than when done completely freehand.

CUTTING DUPLICATE DESIGNS

To make duplicate cut-out designs, mount the foil to be cut between two pieces of hardboard or .040 gauge aluminum secured with tape at the edges, with the design drawn on the top sheet. Drill a series of holes for the blade of the saw to pass through, and proceed as shown in figure 40, which also shows the finished disks, one of which has been modeled.

ETCHING DUPLICATE DESIGNS

An alternate method of making duplicates, by etching, is shown in the same illustration. Only one piece is shown being etched, but for duplicates the design would have to be painted individually in the number of copies desired. A resist against the action of the acid, in this case asphaltum varnish, is used to paint the design and to protect any of the metal not to be etched. An alternate resist is ceresin wax.

When wax is used as a resist coat, the metal to be etched is dipped into heated wax, tipped to drain off excess, then put aside to harden. The design is transferred to the surface of the wax with carbon paper. To

97

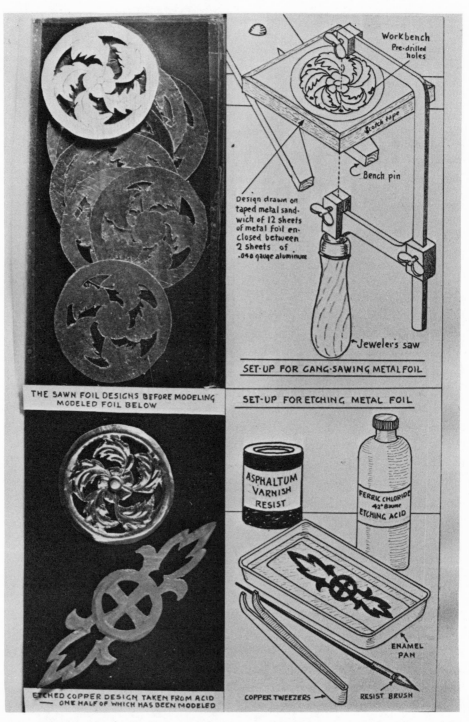

The labels within the figure:

Workbench
Pre-drilled holes
Scotch tape
Bench pin
Design drawn on taped metal sandwich of 12 sheets of metal foil enclosed between 2 sheets of .040 gauge aluminum
Jeweler's saw

SET-UP FOR GANG-SAWING METAL FOIL

THE SAWN FOIL DESIGNS BEFORE MODELING
MODELED FOIL BELOW

SET-UP FOR ETCHING METAL FOIL

ASPHALTUM VARNISH RESIST

FERRIC CHLORIDE 42° Baume ETCHING ACID

ENAMEL PAN

ETCHED COPPER DESIGN TAKEN FROM ACID — ONE HALF OF WHICH HAS BEEN MODELED

COPPER TWEEZERS   RESIST BRUSH

Figure 40. Two methods of producing duplicate designs. **Top:** *By sawing.* **Bottom:** *By etching with acid.*

allow the acid to etch the design, all lines must be scratched through the wax to the bare metal.

The metal to be etched is placed in a shallow plastic or enamel tray, the acid solution (see the section on Etching in chapter 9) poured over it, and the tray rocked from time to time to clear away the bubbles of gas that form on the surface. It is not necessary to watch over the process constantly, but do rock the tray now and then. Etching time varies, with thirty minutes to one hour usually being sufficient for the acid to eat through the foil. The resist must then be removed, using turpentine for asphaltum, or heat for the wax. Rub the metal with fine steel wool.

MAKING MOLDS

LINOLEUM BLOCK MOLDS

A drawing of the proposed design is made and transferred in reverse (in the examples reversal is irrelevant, the designs being symmetrical) to the white surface of a linoleum block. Figure 41, top left, shows a mold in which two different designs (1A and 2A) are cut, using one of the chisels to be found in a set for this purpose.

The cuts are made by using a U-shaped chisel which cuts half-round grooves. Cuts should be evenly made; they are not difficult because linoleum cuts almost like cheese. Apply light pressure on the tool to prevent its slipping, and keep the hand holding the block out of range.

Cut in all of the lines, and if necessary, go over them to smooth out irregularities. This is important if a good positive is to be made.

Cut a piece of foil large enough to encompass all of the design, and place it with the face turned down and flat on the block. Holding it down firmly, rub a spoon-ended tool over its surface to expose the design, then change to a tool with an end to fit the grooves in the mold, and go over all the lines in the design. Do this gently; too much pressure can crack the foil.

Using a flat piece of wood (as the side of a cigar box), flatten the foil, which may tend to be uneven around the design. The first duplicate is now completed, and all that remains to be done is to trim off any excess foil.

Figure 41, 1B, shows a duplicate made of aluminum foil; 1C is a duplicate in copper foil with a fired-on coating of clear flux, which imparts a gold tone to the copper. The reverse side has a fired-on coat of counter-

Figure 41. Two methods of producing duplicate designs. **Left:** *By linoleum block.* **Right:** *By making a wax model and a plaster mold.*

enamel. With a coating on each side the piece is quite stiff enough to be handled without damage. The second duplicate is also produced in both aluminum and copper, the latter being enameled on both sides (2B and 2C). The aluminum foil may be stiffened in any one of the ways previously mentioned for use with aluminum.

PLASTER MOLDS

Another means of making duplicates is by use of a plaster mold taken from an original. This may be a piece of modeled foil, but in the example shown a wax model was first made and then cast.

Making a Wax Model

To model in wax takes skill, but this too can be accomplished with practice. Tools may be bought, but are best made by the modeler who can make them for his particular needs. Figure 42 shows some of the most useful tools for modeling wax. Many modelers make their wax to suit the needs of the job (see Modeling Waxes in chapter 9 for formulas), but it can be bought in craft supply stores.

Figure 41, 3A, shows a seahorse modeled in wax (painted white in the illustration for clarity). First a drawing is made and *transferred in reverse* to a piece of hardboard. Wax is rolled into balls between thumb and first finger, and then pushed onto the sticky surface inside the lines of the design. When the design is completely covered with pressed-down balls, a hot tool is used to smooth the surface, wax being added where necessary.

When an approximate contour has been achieved, the modeling tools are called into play to cut away excess wax to give form to the seahorse. There must be no undercuts on the model, as this would prevent removal of the plaster mold. When completed, the model is given two thin coats of shellac varnish. When dry, a thin coat of oil is applied to prevent the mold from sticking.

Plaster of paris may be used to make the mold, but a harder one may be made by using Durham's Water Putty, used by painters for filling cracks in walls. Follow directions for mixing, which differ from the way plaster is mixed. Build a dike (to contain the plaster) around the edges of the board on which the model sits. Make the mold about one inch thick. Allow it to set up hard (overnight is best). Dry it thoroughly, using a warm oven (250°F.) to speed the process. Look into the cavities of the mold to see if

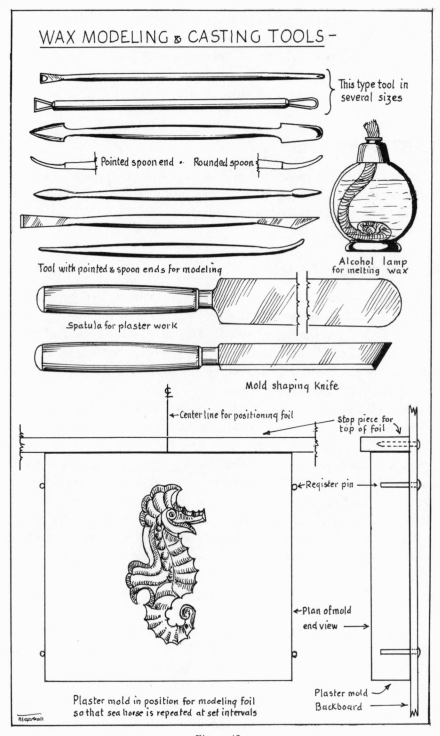

WAX MODELING & CASTING TOOLS -

This type tool in several sizes

Pointed spoon end • Rounded spoon

Tool with pointed & spoon ends for modeling

Alcohol lamp for melting wax

Spatula for plaster work

Mold shaping Knife

←Center line for positioning foil

Stop piece for top of foil ↓

←Register pin

←Plan of mold end view →

Plaster mold Backboard →

Plaster mold in position for modeling foil so that sea horse is repeated at set intervals

Figure 42.

surfaces are clean. If not, take off any irregularities, but be alert to the fact that working on a reversed image can be deceiving.

The completed mold (fig. 41, 3C) shows a seahorse in reverse, sunk instead of raised, as in the original model. It is into the mold that you will model the foil, in the manner already explained. Greater care is necessary with a deeper model, as this is, compared to the mold made in the linoleum block. Copper or brass foils are safer to use in a mold of this kind, but with care and patience aluminum foil can be gently modeled to shape.

After the foil has been modeled to fill the cavities of the mold, it is lifted out. In the example shown, an oval tin lid (3B), is positioned as a form to surround the seahorse, and a tool used to bring out its shape and to make a molded edge, after which the excess foil is trimmed away. A hole is cut at this time if it is to be fitted with a chain when completed.

Being of copper, it may be enameled, which is done by fluxing the face and counter-enameling the back. To add contrast, a background of blue enamel is sifted around the seahorse, and fired in the kiln. The result, a golden seahorse against a background of blue, making a nice pendant to be hung from a chain.

MOLDS FOR MASS PRODUCTION

One method used in industry to duplicate parts is essentially the same as outlined with regard to the making of a model and the casting of a mold. However, there are additional steps to be taken. The point at which the foil has been modeled into the mold is where extra work must be done. Leaving the modeled foil in the mold to leave space for foil at the time of pressing, another mold is made on top of it, being keyed into the lower mold by V-cuts made in the lower mold before the top mold is poured. The molds are then pulled apart and sent to a foundry to be cast in metal. These castings are then trimmed and cleaned up ready to be positioned in a power press. The lower mold is placed in a vise underneath the plunger to which the matching mold is fixed. Careful mating is then assured before the press is operated.

Production can begin by feeding blanks between the molds. In more expensive molds a shaped cutter may be incorporated, so that the pressed items are cut as they leave the press.

This technique for the production of duplicate parts is used in the sign industry, where the foil signs are printed with color or additional text by the lithography process. Also produced by this method are the foil ashtrays seen in airports and restaurants, some quite attractive in design.

WOODEN DIES USED IN DUPLICATING

One other method for duplicating parts uses a wooden die, the design or lettering being carved into its surface. Again, foil is modeled into the cavities of the mold and left there while molten lead is poured over it to form the top mold. Such dies are good for several thousand runs, and are used mainly in the production of advertising signs.

Pressing Out Copies

If a power press is beyond the means of the foilcrafter, the task can be done using a hand-operated screw press, formerly used in offices to copy letters by pressure. Another alternative, an automobile jack placed between a ceiling beam and workbench, will also do the job, but at a slower pace.

FORMS AND MOLDS FOR OTHER PURPOSES

WIRE AS A MOLD MATERIAL (FOR CHAMPLEVÉ)

Dies can be made by soldering wire (bent into a design) onto a back-plate. Foil can then be modeled over this form. For enameling foil, this is an ideal way to form cells into which enamel is placed, the raised design acting as dividers between colors, as in champlevé.

USING FOIL IN THE ROUND

Making a Lamp Base

Figure 43 demonstrates the technique of forming foil over a permanent base of wound cord or rope.

If a lamp base is planned, the necessary electrical components (available from electrical supply houses) should be purchased, and plans formulated for insertion of ends into a base and a top fixture (also avail-

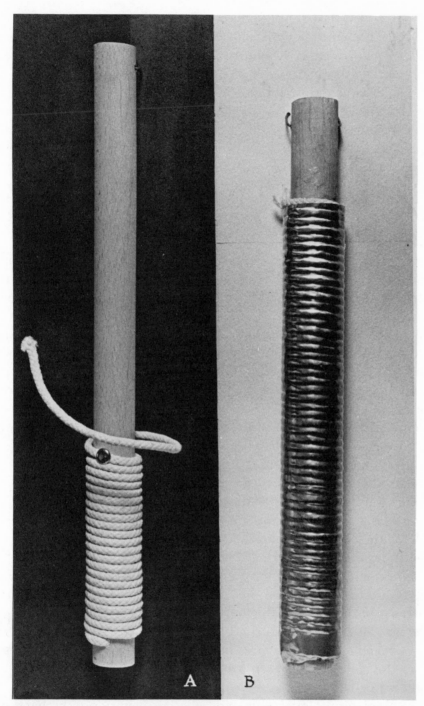

Figure 43. Two steps in the making of a lamp base. **A.** *A cord-wrapped dowel.* **B.** *Foil modeled over the cord-wrapped dowel.*

able from electrical supply houses). Depending upon what is used as a standard, the entire length may have to be split and grooved to accommodate the wiring. At this time drill a hole at each end to secure the ends of the cord as shown in figure 43A at the base of the dowel.

Upon completion of the drilling (and grooving if needed), the standard may be reassembled with glue, and clamped. When the glue has set, coat the entire dowel with glue as a binder (Weldbond is recommended). Glue the end of the cord and insert it in the bottom hole as shown in figure 43A and wind the cord tightly around the entire length of the standard, securing the top end in the hole pre-drilled for that purpose. Clamp the end to hold it in place until the glue sets up.

While waiting for the glue to dry, determine the size of the foil required to cover the cord-wrapped dowel, planning on a butt joint. Cut a strip of foil and wrap it around the cord-wrapped dowel to find its circumference. Cut a piece of foil the desired length, sufficient to cover the windings on the dowel, and as wide as the circumference determined by the strip.

When the cord-wrapped dowel has completely dried, it is ready for covering with foil. Lay the foil flat on a table and coat it with glue (Weldbond). Place the wrapped dowel upon it in the manner of a rolling pin. Bend up one side of the foil around the dowel, press it firmly in place, being sure it is straight. Roll the foil around the dowel until the edges meet. If measurements were accurate, this should be a perfect butt joint, making it less bulky than if it had been overlapped. Hold the foil in place with the aid of tape or rubber bands until the glue sets.

When the glue has dried thoroughly, use a pointed or chisel-edged wooden tool to work the foil down into the cracks between the windings of the cord, keeping the pressure even to assure a unified effect.

When the entire standard has been modeled, add the top fixture and base, and complete the wiring. The lamp is ready to use.

This project may be undertaken with the aid of a lathe as well as by the method outlined. To wind the cord onto the dowel, mount it between centers, coat the dowel with glue, and wrap the cord onto the dowel. The lathe may also be used to form the foil into the spaces between the cords in the modeling step, but care should be taken to hold the forming tool under the spinning dowel to avoid lifting the edge at the butt joint, as might happen if the tool were held as in wood-turning with a chisel.

The final results may be varied, whether being done by hand or by lathe, simply by using different shapes and sizes of rope or even different shapes and sizes of wood on which to wind the material.

BE IMAGINATIVE

Styrofoam may be used as a mold if the design is made in its surface with a hot tool. Wood may also be formed with a wood-burning tool, sold in most craft stores.

Any material that can be carved or molded may be used to make dies for forming metal foils.

MAKING CHRISTMAS ORNAMENTS

At Christmas time and on other holidays there is often a desire for new and different decorations. Ornaments for the Christmas tree or for decorating a room may be produced in quantity by any of the duplicating processes outlined, or they may be cut freehand.

Figure 44 offers suggestions for ornaments, some of which can be produced in quantity, others by cutting folded flat sheets of foil individually. Be creative; make a complete set of original decorations.

Six different patterns are provided, some of which may be used in combination in contrasting foils, as well as graduated sizes. All are relatively simple and can be drawn freehand or traced with the aid of tracing paper from the patterns.

The flowerlike ornament at top may be first made from 3-ply bristol board which can be used as a pattern to scribe around. Inscribe a circle of the desired size and step off its radius around the circumference, which will give six points. Halve the spaces between these points to give center lines for the petals radiating from the center point to beyond the circumference. By trial and error find the center for an arc to form the side of a petal, then repeat until all are drawn in. In use this flower shape may be hung flat from a hole in the top of one petal, or the petals may be turned downward and hung from the center of the circle. Use colored foils for the best effect.

At top left is a pattern for a four-pointed form made in a manner similar to the solids shown in Figure 32 (end closures and molded forms). If made in a series of graduated sizes, these forms may be linked together to form an attractive drop ornament.

First draw a circle of the desired size and inscribe the radii at right angles to each other to produce four points on the circumference. Mark the bottom point as A, and the righthand point B. With AB as radius strike an arc from points A and B to produce center C. Repeat in the other three divisions of the circle. From center C (and the other three centers)

Design for Christmas card foilcrafted in low relief.

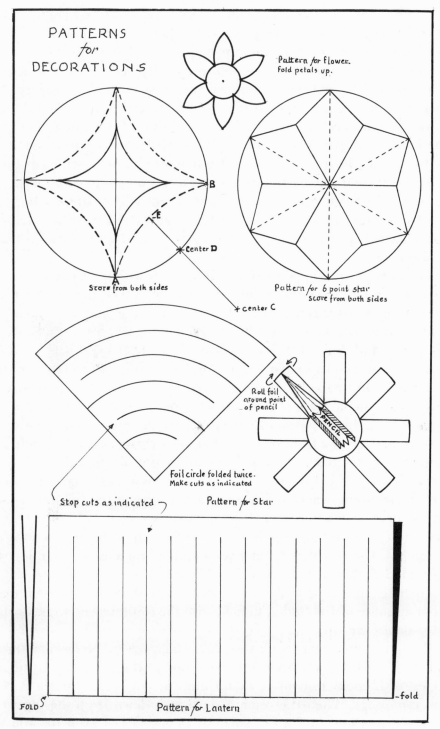

PATTERNS
for
DECORATIONS

Pattern for flower.
fold petals up.

B

E

Center **D**

Score from both sides

center C

Pattern for 6 point star
score from both sides

Roll foil
around point
of pencil

PENCIL

Foil circle folded twice.
Make cuts as indicated

Stop cuts as indicated

Pattern for Star

FOLD

fold

Pattern for Lantern

Figure 44.

with AB as radius strike arcs (from A to B, etc.). With AE as radius and D as center strike an arc as shown. Repeat from the other centers.

Layout may be first made on tracing paper and then transferred to the foil by means of a pointed tool. Remember that solid lines are traced on one side and dotted lines on the reverse side, since the foil is to be bent in two directions. Lines on both sides will be traced in solid (not dotted). When all lines are drawn with a backing of fairly soft material beneath the foil (newspapers or faced corrugated cardboard are suitable), it will be found that the form begins to take shape. This can be helped by finger pressure around the circumference and by pushing the center portion of the foil. Any irregularities may be smoothed out with a flat modeling tool. A wire inserted in a hole at one of the points will serve as a hanger. Graduated shapes may be joined by thin wire so that they twist easily and reflect light.

At top right the six-pointed star is laid out within a circle of the size desired. Step off the radius around the circumference, then connect each step-off mark to the center point. Divide each of the six spaces in half and draw in the lines as shown. Next determine the degree of sharpness of the points and draw in the lines. Again, remember to draw lines on two sides, as indicated by solid or dotted lines. Cut out the star before starting to form it into shape by working alternately from each side to obtain a three-dimensional form. Again, use a flat tool to smooth out the flat surfaces of the points. Insert a wire hanger in a hole in one of the points.

At center left is a form made by folding a cut-out circle of foil first in half, then in quarters, and inscribing arcs from the point, as shown, alternately stopping short of the edge. Cut along these lines with sharp scissors, stopping where indicated. Next, open out the foil into a circle and smooth with a flat tool. Insert a wire and bend at right angles to prevent its removal, then pull the cut sections apart to form a dangling ornament. Use of colored foil gives an added dimension, with one side colored, the other silver.

The pattern for the basket or lantern shape shown at bottom is made from a square of foil folded in half, with the resulting rectangle divided into equal parts, lines stopping short of the top. Cut along these lines, stopping the cuts where indicated. Now open out to the original square but do not smooth flat. Bend the foil into a cylinder and join the two edges (with epoxy cement or by turning the edges back on themselves and crimping). When the cement sets, push down from the top while resting the cylinder on a flat surface. If pressure is even the foil will assume a shape wide at the center, with the cut strips assuming a curved shape. Any irregularities can be smoothed out with a flat tool. To hang, insert a looped wire into holes made in opposite sides of the top. A light bulb placed inside will make the ornament into a lantern.

The remaining pattern is for an eight-pointed star, the size of which is determined by the outer circle. The inner circle is marked off into eight spaces by trial and error, using a pair of dividers. The parts that will form the points of the star are drawn in using a T-square and 45° triangle through the points marked off around the circumference. If a number of stars are to be made, draw the design on bristol board to make a scribing pattern. Cut the foil to shape and then, using a short piece of sharpened pencil, fold the foil around the cone of the sharpened end. By using a short pencil it is easier to form the remaining points. Suspend the star from a thin wire passing through two points, with a bend at the bottom to keep it in place.

Chapter 6

SPINNING AND ALTERNATE METHODS OF FORMING FOIL

The term "spinning" as applied to metalworking tends to be confusing, conjuring up visions of a cloth of gold spun from metal threads, but such is not the case. The term merely describes the action of the rotating lathe in which is mounted a chuck (form), over which metal is spun to take the shape of that mold.

SPINNING FORMS ON A LATHE

As a method for forming metals, the craft of spinning is said to have originated in China, the country that gave the world the magnetic compass, fine porcelain, and regrettably, gunpowder. Both the Greeks and the Romans spun plates by this method, using the relatively soft pewter for that purpose. Spinning was known in England in the 14th century, although how it was done on a "pole" lathe is hard to imagine.

A modern lathe has a continuous forward motion, but the lathes of the 14th century were reciprocating, action being accomplished by wrapping a rope around a mandrel mounted in the lathe, which was tied to a springy sapling (pole) over the lathe and to a foot treadle underneath; hence the term pole lathe. As the technique is described, it will become apparent why spinning would be more difficult to accomplish on such a primitive contraption.

As a means of stiffening foil, spinning is ideal, the metal assuming bowl or plate forms into which a stiffening bead can be spun. It is possible only to give a general concept of the craft of spinning, but anyone interested in knowing more about it or taking up the craft should consult books on the subject, some of which include designs.

ESSENTIALS OF SPINNING

A series of diagrams shown in figure 45 will be helpful in grasping the principles of spinning. At top (A) is a lathe seen from the rear, on the bed of which are mounted headstock, tool rest, and tailstock. In the tool rest a bar is clamped in which are set three upright steel spindles, between which the shaping tools are placed. The lathe is belt-driven by a motor;

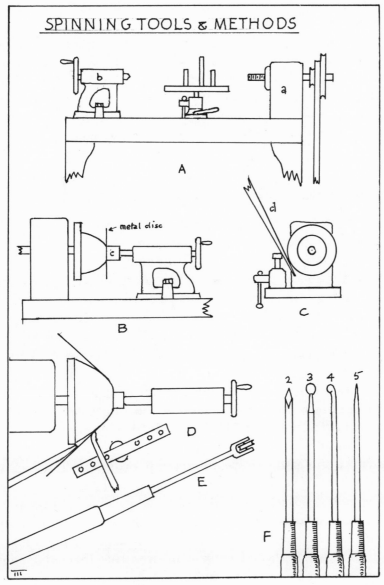

Figure 45.

speed of rotation is regulated by changing the belt on the stepped pulleys.

In B the lathe is shown set up for spinning a bowl over a wooden chuck, the foil being positioned on the chuck, and held in place by a follow block, which can be tightened by a turn of the wheel on the tailstock.

In order to have the foil disk spin true, the lathe is rotated slowly while a wooden stick is held lightly against its edge. (C shows an end-on view to make this clear.) When the disk runs true, the tailstock wheel is given a slight twist to tighten the follow block.

Spinning is accomplished in a series of steps to gradually shape the metal to the form of the chuck. In D several of these steps have already been performed. A steel (or wood) spinning tool is then placed between the upright spindle and the disk, and pressure is applied to further form the metal to the chuck. The spinning tools (E and F) are typical of those used, but there are other shapes and sizes for particular needs.

Finishing a Spun Form

When the foil assumes the total form of the chuck, the excess metal is either cut off with the diamond-headed cutter (F2) or enough metal is left to form a bead by turning over the edge and folding it under.

There are instances, particularly when using heavier gauge metals, when the spinning must cease while the piece is annealed by heating it to redness and then cooling it to make it soft and to prevent cracking. Some industrial spinning lathes are equipped with heating torches that play on the metal that is being spun. This must be done over steel chucks, as wood will burn.

The tools used in spinning are mostly made of steel, with ends shaped to perform specific tasks. They are mounted in long wooden handles that fit under the arm of the operator, for much leverage is required to force the metal to conform to the chuck.

As described, this is simple spinning, but in order to make shapes such as a coffee pot, the chucks are made to collapse when a pin is removed. The making of such chucks is a highly skilled operation, as is the spinning over them. Few amateur craftworkers attempt to make these industrial types of chucks, but simple forms are easy to make by anyone who can do turning on a lathe. It should be remembered that forms for spinning should have rounded corners, as metal tends to crack when forced into tight places.

USEFUL ITEMS EASY TO MAKE

Half-spheres are easy to turn, and two placed together with a flange left on for soldering make a decorative top for a flagpole. Foil so spun could be used on a Christmas tree, being much stronger than the glass balls customarily used. Small bowls, candle cups, ashtrays, and small plates are suitable projects for the foilcraft worker who is fortunate enough to own a lathe.

ALTERNATE FORMING METHODS

For those who consider spinning as too mechanical and far removed from forming by hand, there are conventional ways to shape metal. Many object to the marks left on the metal by the spinning tools, an example of which may be seen in cookware produced by this means. These marks are regarded by the makers as part of the process of forming a utensil; they are too costly to remove, and to do so would make the metal thinner and weaker.

HAND-FORMING OBJECTS

To form a bowl by hand requires special tools in the form of mallets and hammers of various shapes and sizes, plus an assortment of stakes over which the metal is formed. While it is fascinating to see a bowl in the process of formation, the task is hard and long. Moreover, it takes skill to produce an even bowl—one without distortions, and that sits flat when set on its rim. Such a craft is best learned under a master craftsman, or at a school teaching the subject.

It is possible to form foil into rounded shapes by using a wooden block with a slight depression in its top. Hammers are not used, since they stretch metal, and foil is already of light gauge. Small wooden mallets are suitable, but rubbing around in circles toward the center will also shape the foil. It takes a long time to get any depth, so this method is best used just for doming foil to add strength.

Wood and metal molds are available in which foils can be modeled; however, the trick with them is to try to prevent the metal from creasing and being ruined. Do not use deep forms; the foil will crack before total shape is achieved. Small shallow trays are the best to use; edges may, with care, be turned over to form a bead (even over wire), but it is a slow process to be done only as a challenge.

Chapter 7

LOOKING INTO REPOUSSÉ AND CASTING

The craft of repoussé and the art produced by this metalworking technique is ancient in origin, and is still practiced today in the countries of the Middle East, where it is thought to have originated. It is a demanding craft practiced worldwide by both professionals and amateurs, requiring great skill in the use of hammers and a wide assortment of metal punches. A noisy craft, it is unsuited to residential areas.

Anyone transferring from modeling metal foils to repoussé work will find that the change from gauges of 33-38 to 20-22 is considerable. The latter gauges are those commonly used in repoussé work. Foils are an easy way to produce low-relief work, but for high relief it is necessary to switch to repoussé and different techniques. The change is worthwhile even if projects are kept small. There is great satisfaction in making metal bend to one's will under the blows of a hammer, or in revealing form by use of punches.

Figures 46 and 47 are examples of ancient repoussé work from the Metropolitan Museum of Art in New York. They were chosen from dozens of prints on file, one rather simple in technique, the other being intricately detailed. Both show surfaces enriched by the use of punches and chasing tools.

COPPER IN REPOUSSÉ

Repoussé literally means "pushing out," which is the process of hammering metal, usually copper, from the back to produce forms—orna-

Figure 46. Early sixteenth-century German brass repoussé dish.—Photograph courtesy of the Metropolitan Museum of Art, gift of W. L. Hildburgh, 1932.

mental, human, or animal—and refining detail from the front by use of metal punches called tracers and chasing tools, the latter adding texture to surfaces.

Work in this medium is often confused with a casting unless picked up and handled, because repoussé objects are lighter in weight. Experts can usually tell at a glance the difference between the two by the enriched surface treatment possible with the repoussé technique, chiseled and chased areas catching the light. A study of these techniques is well worth the time, and many of the bigger art museums have a wide range of examples from many countries.

Figure 47. Sixteenth-century Italian steel repoussé plaquette. Allegory of David and Saul.—Photograph courtesy of the Metropolitan Museum of Art, Rogers Fund, 1950.

TOOLS NEEDED

Figure 48, bottom half, shows but a few of the tools used by the repoussé craftsperson. A craft supply catalog will give a better idea of the multitude of tracing and chasing tools used for detail work.

Hammers of various kinds and weights are used to shape the metal, but the chasing hammer used to drive the punches has a distinctive shape, with a large face, a very springy handle, and a bulbous handgrip. A 16-ounce hammer is used for the larger punches, and a 4-ounce one for the chasing tools.

Large repoussé work is seldom produced today, most craftworkers preferring smaller projects. One artist, Saul Baizerman (1889-1957), produced many full-sized human figures by this method. His work is worth studying to see how he pushed the medium to extremes to produce his sculptures. No other artist has followed in his footsteps, nor are any likely to do so in this age of non-representational art.

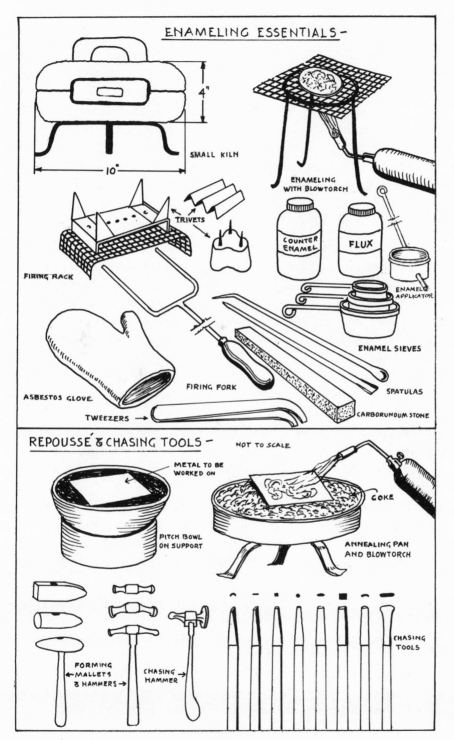

ENAMELING ESSENTIALS—

4"

10"

SMALL KILN

ENAMELING WITH BLOWTORCH

TRIVETS

COUNTER ENAMEL

FLUX

ENAMEL APPLICATOR

FIRING RACK

ENAMEL SIEVES

ASBESTOS GLOVE

FIRING FORK

SPATULAS

TWEEZERS →

CARBORUNDUM STONE

REPOUSSÉ & CHASING TOOLS—

NOT TO SCALE

METAL TO BE WORKED ON

COKE

PITCH BOWL ON SUPPORT

ANNEALING PAN AND BLOWTORCH

FORMING MALLETS & HAMMERS →

CHASING HAMMER →

CHASING TOOLS

Figure 48.

DESIGNING REPOUSSÉ

Before starting to work, make a sketch of the project, fully detailed so that all intricacies are apparent, because it will be referred to constantly during the progress of the work.

Cut out the metal and pass it through an acid dip (see section on Pickle in chapter 9), to make a clean surface onto which to transfer the drawing. Placing the drawing face-down over carbon paper on the metal, trace in all lines of the form. Because lines might be rubbed out while working, scribe them in lightly with a sharp-ended tool.

POSITIONING THE WORK

Although Baizerman beat his forms from unsupported copper, the general technique is to beat the metal against a pitch bowl on a support, such as that illustrated in figure 48. A bowl or flat pan is used to contain the pitch, depending on the size and shape of the metal to be worked on. The resiliency of the pitch may be conditioned by applied heat, its composition varying according to the weather—cold tending to make it too hard, summer heat too soft. Various materials may be added to counteract these conditions. A light coat of oil is applied to the surface that is to be turned down, to prevent its sticking to the pitch too tightly, causing removal to be difficult.

Heat is applied to the surface of the pitch, just enough to soften it to allow adhesion. Place the oiled side of the metal on the pitch, heating its surface just enough to assure that its coolness does not harden the pitch underneath.

Work may begin, and this is usually done from the center, working outwards. No two craftsmen work alike, and some like to work on the front of a panel to set in the design by use of tracing tools. Others work exclusively from the back, leaving the tracing until later, when the metal is turned over. The main idea is to have the design progress overall, not just in one place. This assures that strains caused by hammering are equally distributed over the surface of the metal.

It is important that the metal to be worked on is well-seated on the pitch, especially as work progresses, when all depressions made must be filled with pitch to avoid accidental denting by the hammer. As the metal is beaten and formed it becomes brittle, and must be removed from the pitch for annealing, or softening. This is done with a blowtorch, heating to redness and allowing the metal to cool, when it is again soft and pliable. An annealing pan is shown in figure 48.

Assuming that work was begun on the back, and all work is completed that can be done from this side, remove the metal from the pitch; anneal it, fill the depressions with pitch, and put it back onto the pitch back-side down.

Using a tracing tool between thumb and first finger, incline it backward a little so that a corner of the tool digs in, and tap it with the hammer. A chasing tool is held angled slightly towards oneself and tapped with the lighter hammer. Work is usually done from the center outward, but again, some repoussé workers have their own ways of doing things, best suited to their convenience or as reflections of their training and past experience.

If after working from the front it is found that more relief is needed in certain parts of the work, the metal is again annealed and set onto the pitch face down. The annealing is especially important, because to add to the relief means working with metal already stretched thin. One too many blows could then crack the metal, ruining hours of patient work. A crack can be brazed, but the scarred area may then take on a dissimilar color when the piece is being patined (chemically colored).

Satisfied that the piece is properly modeled and detail is fully traced onto the front, the chasing tools are used to give either a textured surface to the background, or to cut in highlights that will enhance the details. This can be a very long process if a piece is large, because every square inch of background should be textured. If there is foliage in the design, each leaf or blossom may receive highlighting in the form of chiseled facets.

The test of any repoussé craftsperson lies in the knowing of precisely when to stop, for too much toolwork may detract rather than enhance the work.

NEARLY A LOST ART

While apprenticed to the art metal trade in England, the author had experience with repoussé techniques as practiced commercially. The architects for Selfridge's Department Store in London wished to decorate the elevator enclosures with panels of classical design executed in the repoussé technique. Such work done individually would be too costly, and castings were deemed too heavy to use on the sliding elevator doors. It was suggested that models be made in wax from which iron molds could be made, and the metal beaten into them. Because there were several doors of similar design, this was the method chosen (see fig. 49).

Figure 49. Modern repoussé work on the elevator enclosure at Selfridge's in London.

The cost of this project, even done as outlined, proved too high for continued use, so that when work of this kind was commissioned the panels were stamped out in a power press, in iron molds made from wax models. As this example shows, in days past cost was no consideration, but the work of handcraftsmen is now too costly to use commercially. This is why skills become lost, as crafts one by one decline because of cost factors.

In recent years there has been a movement back to old crafts, particularly smithing, ceramics, and weaving. Such crafts may be able to pay their way by demand for their products, but metalworking by hand is so costly that only a few can afford articles produced in this way.

Although foil modeling and repoussé differ widely in their techniques, this outline of repoussé procedures may stimulate interest in that craft, a logical progression. Who knows? A new Cellini may emerge to spark another Renaissance.

WORKING REPOUSSÉ IN LEAD

Although details may not be as sharp as in copper, consideration should be given to working in lead, using some of the repoussé techniques on this soft and pliable metal. The pounding may be done against sand in place of pitch, with wet sand being used to fill cavities before working from the front. The dull thud of mallet on lead may be less damaging to hearing than the crash of hammer on copper.

In days when lead was cheap it was used to cover roofs and to make cisterns to catch the water that ran off them. Many ancient examples of the use of lead may be seen in Europe, where church roofs are still in place after centuries, as are cisterns; but wars have often destroyed lead artifacts, either because they were melted down for use in munitions, or demolished by bombs. One is reminded of the use of lead as a weapon by an old cry: "The enemy is at our gates, but the lead is on the boil."

Although many modern craftsmen use pewter as a metal with which to work, lead is still used to make garden pools and cast statuary. Few plumbers use it since the advent of brass, copper, and plastic plumbing supplies; so its use is open to those who like to work in a metal that bends and forms easily, and lasts forever. However, because of possible leaching, at no time should lead be used to form utensils intended for food or beverages.

TOOLS AND MATERIALS

Necessary tools for working in lead are tinsnips, a strong-bladed knife, a few shaped-head mallets, a ball-peen hammer or two (of different weights), and if surface decorations are to be made, a few punches and blunt cold chisels. A soldering iron, solder, and flux are also needed for making seams.

Lead may be purchased by the square foot (in sheets of different thicknesses), and by the pound (in pigs), to be used in casting. A supply of six-pound sheet lead will be needed for first projects. Thicker lead and antimonial lead may be used for such projects that need to be strong.

Lead may be used in combination with other metals for aesthetic reasons, but not with aluminum, for not only is the latter too much like new lead in color, but it does not last long when in contact with lead.

FORMING A GARDEN POOL

To form lead it is best to bend it over shapes made of wood. A shallow pool may be formed against a frame constructed of 2″ x 4″ wood in the required size. Curves in the frame are produced by planing.

A round pool may be made from a flat sheet, the edges being scalloped to disguise the deformation that occurs around its perimeter. Square corners may simply butt, and be soldered to seal the crack where edges meet.

After a few projects have been completed, ways of forming will be almost self-evident, or may be devised or improvised on the job. A large soldering iron of the torch-heated variety is best to use, because the electric soldering guns are intended for smaller work. A blowtorch or plumber's stove is needed to heat the iron, the tip of which must always be kept clean and free from grease, and flux is applied just before the iron is brought into play. Neat soldering takes practice, but be patient for great globs of solder add nothing to the beauty of a project.

Decoration can take many forms. The center of a panel may be enhanced by weaving strips of lead to form a rectangle, and surrounding it with a flat frame. This can be soldered in place. Top seams may be made by bending the lead over onto itself, or they may be rolled over a dowel or half-round molding, then pulled free at the end. Lines may be scratched in with a knife, or punched in with a wide, blunt-ended cold chisel. Punches may be made or bought as needed. Metals used for decoration may be riveted to the lead or tacked in place with a soldering iron.

OUTDOOR ACCESSORIES OF LEAD

Lead is a good metal to use for outdoor lanterns and mailboxes, but both may need some stiffening device such as angle-iron. The mailbox may be of wood covered with lead sheet, or a standard type of box may be so covered. When nailing lead to wood, make square lead washers to fit on the nails; these can then be formed into a decorative head by bending them over the top. Lead rosettes may be made and soldered over screw heads to hide them.

CASTING LEAD STATUARY

Lead is easy to cast into any type of mold, even plaster, so long as it is *bone dry* before the lead is poured. If wet it will produce steam which may make the mold blow up, causing injury.

If much casting is contemplated, a plumber's stove is best for melting the lead, but a blowtorch will suffice. Several sizes of ladles are needed for melting and pouring the lead. As it melts, a scum forms on top which must be skimmed off, leaving the metal looking shiny. The lead should not be overheated—just fluid enough to pour easily.

Molds used should be warmed to prevent the lead from chilling before it gets into the detailed parts of the mold. Lead too hot will scorch the mold, and surfaces will not be smooth.

Casting a statue of any significant size is a job for a lead caster, because special molds and casting techniques are used in producing statues, but a small animal sculpture is not beyond the skill of an amateur, nor is the making of a mold. For this type of mold (in the round), known as a piece mold, plaster of paris may be used, but there are other products that withstand heat better.

A mold must have vent holes for the escape of air and gases, and a wide mouth to allow the lead to enter. If the cast is to be hollow, the lead is poured, swirled around in the mold, and then poured off. This is known as slush-molding. It takes practice, but is not difficult or dangerous if proper care is taken to avoid the molten metal as it pours from the mold. Further details and procedures will be found in books dealing specifically with casting techniques.

Chapter 8

TECHNIQUES OF ENAMELING ON COPPER FOIL

Of all the methods for adding firmness to foils, there is one that is ideal for copper foil only, and that is by fusing vitreous enamels onto back and front. Brass and aluminum foils are unsuited for this treatment, their melting points being lower than that of the enamels.

Copper foil, being light in weight, is ideal for making jewelry, especially when it is enameled. Moreover, if enameled back and front at the same time, no distortion will take place. If doming is given to a circular piece of foil it may then be enameled on only the front side without producing distortion, but both sides of any other piece must be enameled to prevent distortion.

EQUIPMENT NEEDED

To take advantage of this method of stiffening foil, no more equipment is needed than that shown in figure 48, top. The gadget to the right of the flux bottle was devised for depositing enamels into tight spaces. The uses for the various items shown are described as techniques are explained.

PRACTICAL EXPERIENCE

Enameling techniques are not difficult to learn to apply, but the beginner is advised to practice the simpler techniques for some time before advancing to the more sophisticated methods used by professional enamelists and the mass-manufacturers of jewelry, badges, and trophies.

Figure 50.   Holiday decorations made of foil.

SIMPLE ENAMELING

CLEANING THE METAL

Copper when purchased is likely to be slightly oxidized, and must be cleaned before it is enameled, either by an acid dip (see section on Pickle in chapter 9), an acid substitute (Sparex II); or abrasion with steel wool or pumice powder. It is then washed in running water, and handled only by its edges to avoid being marred by fingerprints, which may be oily.

Figure 51. Foilcrafted enameled fish on a coral base.

The copper to be enameled is placed back-side up on a trivet of appropriate size, and painted with gum (tragacanth), on which the powdered enamel will stick. Counter enamel is placed in a sieve and sprinkled over the damp surface. The piece is then turned face up on the trivet, and gum applied to this side, which is then sprinkled with clear flux. Place both the trivet and the piece on a firing rack, and set it aside to air-dry. (Premature firing would produce steam which may bubble the enamel, so be sure it is thoroughly dry.)

When dry, the whole assembly is lifted on the firing fork and placed in the kiln for several minutes, or until the powdered enamel glazes over, which is the signal for removing it from the kiln. The fired piece should be immediately placed in a draft-free place for cooling. (Rapid cooling or a draft could cause the enamel to flake off.) The fired piece should now be a golden color on its face, and neutral gray-green on the back.

As may be seen, this simple process produces limited results, but it does stiffen the copper foil, which is all that is promised from this technique.

CHAMPLEVÉ AND CLOISONNÉ

In order to include colors, provision must be made to keep each separate, which may be accomplished in any one of several ways. Engraving or etching out cavities in the metal is known as champlevé. The forming of spaces with wire, either silver-soldered to a base or fused in place with clear flux (as used in simple enameling), is known as cloisonné.

These are the techniques most frequently mentioned when enameling is discussed; if the preparation of the metal for these two techniques is impossible, the freehand placing of enamels may have to be resorted to, or stencils may be used.

If unskilled with a graving tool, it is not advisable to attempt to chisel out a design in copper in order to form the cells for holding enamels. Even silver-soldering a wire design onto the work is not easy, although firing it on with flux is a simpler way to do it. The foil modeler is more fortunate, inasmuch as dividing lines may be tooled into the copper to form cells or designs.

APPLICATION OF ENAMEL

Freehand enameling, in which one color of enamel is laid next to another with no metal in between, requires a steady hand and patience, plus multiple firings in the kiln.

An alternate method is to cut a stencil for each color laid on, then fired, one by one until all are in place. By cutting out a hole or design in thin card, the enamel can be placed through it to take its shape. If the edges around the hole are gummed, no enamel will spill where it is not supposed to be. If using both hard and soft enamels in this process, the hard ones should be fired first; softer ones in subsequent firing.

Placing the enamels in a freehand manner is accomplished by first gumming an area in which a color is to go, then putting the enamel onto that surface with a series of spatulas, sized to the space.

With a small paintbrush handy, edges can be trued up, or spilled enamel brushed off.

A small cup might be devised, made of a bottle cap in which a thin tube is inserted near the bottom. A wire handle is fastened at the top. In use the cup is half-filled with enamel, then tapped with the forefinger to make it flow from the tube in a controllable amount. This has been found ideal for laying in areas of enamel, and superior to spatula application. It is possible to lay all colors at one time if great care is taken to avoid overspill, but it is safer to fire each color separately.

REFIRING

It may sometimes be necessary to refire a piece to add more enamel to parts of the design, causing no difficulty if gum is brushed only onto the areas to be so treated. When this is necessary in champlevé or cloisonné enameling, the copper dividers will have to be cleaned of oxide by rubbing them with a carborundum stone under running water. This may scratch surrounding enamels, but when refired they will smooth out.

ADDING A FREEHAND DESIGN

If a piece has been enameled with one color as a background and a freehand design is required in its center, the best way to do this is to mix with glycerine a color that will contrast with the background, to make a sort of ink. Using this on a brush, paint in the design, then sieve enamel over it, let it dry, and fire it. The glycerine will burn off without harming the enamel. If several colors are called for, draw each color, fire, then repeat as often as necessary. (This same technique can be accomplished with fine enamels mixed in gum water colored as for the glycerine method.)

SWIRLING

One other technique used in enameling is known as swirling. Small lumps of enamel are laid in place usually on an enameled background, using any colors desired in combination. A very hot kiln is required, for the lumps must become pasty before they are manipulated by the use of a swirling iron, a long rod with a turned-down, pointed end.

It is necessary to wear an asbestos glove while swirling because the heat is intense. When the enamels are ready, the kiln door is opened and the iron is inserted to swirl the molten enamels. This is a hit-or-miss operation, but results are often surprising and pleasing, well-suited for jewelry pendants and earrings.

OTHER TECHNIQUES

One other method of making a design against a background is to paint the copper overall with Scale-Off (available at craft suppliers), then scratch the design into its surface before it dries completely, exposing the copper beneath. Place enamels in the scratched-out spaces, either dry or over gum, let dry, then fire. When taken from the kiln the Scale-Off will do just that, leaving bright copper exposed, against which the design appears in contrast. This, in essence, is another method of stenciling.

For the beginner the opaque enamels are safer to use. The transparent and opalescent types are a little harder to handle, and are used for special effects. Try out the different types of enamel on scrap copper before attempting to make serious use of them.

A more difficult enameling technique is called plique-à-jour, in which a filigree of wire or pierced copper has enamel suspended in the spaces or holes, without backing of any kind. It is not easy to do, nor is it appropriate unless the finished piece is to be suspended against the light, when it is similar in effect to a stained glass window. All enamels used are transparent. There is little point in describing it further; mention of the technique being made only to familiarize the novice with the term. This is also true for Limoges enameling, which is a painting technique used when scenes are painted on an enameled surface. Both procedures are frequently used by professionals.

All of the enameling techniques listed are intended for use on any surface: flat pieces, objects in the round, or upright, as in the sides of a box. All but the flat work requires special equipment for suspending the works being fired, and should be left for the experienced craftsperson.

Many of the fine vases, lamps, and caskets seen in museum exhibits of enamelware were made by the champlevé or cloisonné techniques, the former type also featuring engraved or chased ornamentation on the metal parts comprising the cells into which the enamel is placed.

Chapter 9

ADDITIONAL FORMULAS, PRODUCTS, AND PROCEDURES

There remain a few ideas and suggestions that may prove of interest to craftspersons. Not always easy to find when needed even when a library is nearby, a collection of eclectic miscellany for the metalcrafter is presented as an aid to greater achievement.

GILDING

When gold was first discovered there was no technology for rolling it into sheets, but fire was used to melt it so that it could be poured into ingots, which were then beaten into sheets of foil. From these sheets were made masks and priestly or royal ornaments, such as those found in Egypt. Not content with thin foil, the craftsmen beat it even thinner into leaves, as they are now called, which today may be bought in books 3½ x 3½ inches, interleaved with tissue. This leaf is only about five-millionths of an inch thick (thin), and is available in deep rich gold of 23½ karat, lemon gold of 18½ karat, and pale gold of 16 karat. Leaf is also available in silver and aluminum, the latter often being used in place of silver because it does not become black with time as does silver.

These metallic leaves can be used for gilding on a large scale or for minor touch-up of damaged gilt frames. It is far better than so-called gold paint, which is really bronze powder suspended in a vehicle such as japan varnish. The technique of gilding is an ancient one, much used by monks of the Middle Ages for heightening the ornamental parts of illuminated manuscripts.

It is not difficult to learn how to gild, but it does take practice to be good at it. It also takes good judgment to know just when to lay the leaf in place.

The gold leaf used to gild domes of public buildings and the balls atop flagpoles is a special 23-karat type called "patent." When laid, this leaf does not bear close inspection, the leaf often being imperfect, containing small holes or cracks.

Goldleafing is a useful accomplishment to attain, and the foil worker can make use of it for highlighting modeled ornament, as an alternative to cutting gold foil and glueing it in place.

Gold leaf may be applied to any smooth, hard surface such as glass, metal, or varnished wood. It can also be used on parchment or vellum, as in illuminated manuscripts. The gold leaf used for signs on glass is the most perfect. The so-called "surface" gold may have imperfections, and is also a little cheaper.

Gold leaf is applied over a thin coating of size, of which there are two kinds, japan and gelatin, the latter being used for gilding vellum. Japan goldsize dries quickly, and when tacky, the leaf is laid over it. Artists use egg white when incorporating gold in their paintings, but this causes a bad smell when old.

The gilder uses a palette padded with cotton, over which suede is tacked. On this with a rather blunt knife, he cuts his leaf to size. If working outdoors the palette is fitted with a windshield at one end. Leaf is transferred from book to palette by use of a wide, thinly haired brush, called a tip. For burnishing the leaf when completely set, an agate- or polished steel-ended tool is used.

When applying gold leaf on vellum, the gelatin size, called water size, is used. Raised portions of a design, as in an initial letter, are made by applying gesso (a mixture of whiting and gum) to form a hard, smooth surface on which to lay the gold leaf. Much of the decorated parts of designs on manuscripts are in red, which contrasts nicely with the gold. This type of gilding is a high art, requiring much practice and a steady hand.

Leaf may be laid on a surface that has been given a coat of goldsize, but no matter which type is used, it must be allowed to get tacky before leaf is put upon it. Laid on too soon, the leaf may wrinkle, making later burnishing impossible. If the size gets dry, the leaf will not adhere.

It is wise when first attempting gilding to practice with size on small areas that will not use much leaf. Do this with different combinations of goldsize and surfaces. When assured that proficiency has been attained, work may start on a larger job.

Before tipping the leaf onto it, the pad should be dusted with talcum powder to prevent its sticking to the leather. Cut to size, just slightly larger than the area to be gilded. Save the waste as it may be traded back to the dealer when more is purchased; also small snippets of leaf often come in handy for small jobs, especially on jewelry, for highlighting.

Gold when freshly laid is semi-matt but may be made bright by rubbing carefully with an agate or steel burnisher. Do this gently or the leaf may rupture. One special finish often used by sign writers is mottling the surface of the laid leaf in an all-over pattern. This is done with a chamois-tipped tool by twisting between thumb and first finger. It takes practice to make a neat pattern.

Before attempting gilding, visit a sign shop and watch a professional at work. More can be learned by watching than by experimenting. The sign artist may also have information on where to buy goldsize and books of leaf. Knowing the right stage of tackiness of the goldsize before leaf is laid is important, and this might also be learned by watching the professional at work.

ETCHING

The practice of using acids or alkalies to etch metals is centuries old, and processes have been refined over the years. Today many industrial parts are made in this way, particularly in the electronics field in the production of printed circuits; metal dies and nameplates are also produced in this way.

Etching is an aid to the foilcrafter in the duplication of components. All surfaces must first be coated with asphaltum varnish or wax (ordinary paraffin wax will do), the design being transferred onto the coated surface. The design must be scratched through to the bare metal, being careful not to remove the coating from any surface not to be etched.

A bit of liquid detergent added to the solution will relieve surface tension and allow the acid to work on the metal's surface.

During the etching process, take the metal from the acid periodically and rinse in water; replace in acid bath. Repeat until sufficiently etched. In handling the objects in the acid solution, use copper tongs or rubber gloves. Always rinse thoroughly. When etching is completed, rinse, wash in soap and water, and dry.

ETCH FOR ALUMINUM

Formula #1

Water	40 oz.
Alcohol	4 oz.
Butter of (or chloride of) antimony	4 oz.

Combine the first three ingredients and add:

Acetic acid	6 oz.

Formula #2

Water	1 gal.
Ammonia	¾ oz.
Copper sulphate	2½ g.
Sodium hydroxide (caustic soda)	7 oz.

Combine first four ingredients and add:

75% phosphoric acid	1 to 2 drops

Formula #3

Water	1 oz., liquid measure

Add perchloride of iron (an acid) 1 oz., liquid measure

ETCH FOR BRASS

Mix solutions *A* and *B* to produce the etching fluid.

Solution *A*

Water	100 parts
Add nitric acid	16 parts

Solution *B*

Water	100 parts
Potassium chlorate	6 parts

ETCH FOR COPPER

Formula #1

Water	5 parts

Add nitric or sulphuric acid 1 part

Formula #2

Water	5 parts
Potassium bichromate (saturated solution)	2 parts

Add nitric acid or sulphuric acid 1 part

Formula #3

Water	32 oz.
Bichromate of potash	3 oz.

Add concentrated sulphuric acid 3 oz.

ETCH FOR SILVER

Water	1 pt.
Isopropyl alcohol (any strength)	¼ pt.
Add nitric acid	1¼ pts.

Use at a temperature of 75°F.

TO ETCH OR FROST STEEL

Copper sulphate	1 oz.
Alum	½ oz.
Salt	¼ oz.

Mix with ¼ pt. vinegar.

Add nitric acid	20 drops

MODEL MAKING

In days past a craftsman learned from his master how to compound formulas used in a particular craft. It is now possible to purchase ready-mixed compounds, obviating the need to keep on hand a variety of chemicals and other materials. However, for those who still prefer to mix their own, several modeling wax formulas are listed.

How well a wax works depends on the temperature of the studio in which it is used; this is why formulas for both hard and soft waxes are given.

MODELING WAXES

Formula #1

Beeswax	2 lbs.
Venice turpentine	4½ oz.
Lard	2 oz.
Color	2 lbs.

Mix together all ingredients except color in a double boiler (either Pyrex or enamel), and place over heat until melted. Stir, then add color and stir again.

Caution: Never place a wax formula in direct contact with heat; always use a double boiler, and watch the mixture carefully as it is highly flammable.

Formula #2
  (A fairly soft formula)

Beeswax	1 lb.
Cornstarch	8 oz.
Venice turpentine	4 oz.
Olive oil	1 oz.

Mix as **Formula #1** and melt the mixture. Then add:

Color (dry, powdered)	1½ lbs.

Formula #3 (A harder mixture)

Beeswax	2½ lbs.
Japanese wax	1½ lbs.
Carnauba wax	¼ lb.
Paraffin wax	6 oz.
Venice turpentine	¼ lb.
Lard	½ lb.
Olive oil	4 fl. oz.

Mix as **Formula #1** and melt the mixture. Then add:

Color (dry, powdered)	1½ lbs.

SURFACE TREATMENT OF METALS

Much of the beauty of metals depends on the surface treatment given to a finished work, be it a casting or a project made of sheet metal. The coloring or antiquing of metals is a fine art in which chemicals and heat treatment play a large part. Most sculptors leave this process to specialists who do nothing else. This does not mean, however, that it is beyond the average craftsperson who wishes to add beauty to a piece of finished work.

Included here are some of the standard formulas used by professionals. They are time-tested, but results obtained depend on the skill of the person using them.

PICKLE: THE PROCESS OF REMOVING OXIDES FROM METALS

The first task, before coloring is attempted, is to get the metal clean and bright. This is done with acids, which should be handled very carefully to avoid skin burns.

Because these are all quick-acting, do not leave the metal in any longer than is necessary to get it clean and bright.

For Cleaning Silver, Copper, and Brass

Water	10 parts
Sulphuric acid	1 part

Use hot for best results, and handle the metal with copper tongs, or wear rubber gloves when removing the metal from the acid. Rinse carefully.

> *When mixing formulas containing acid, always add acid to water, never the reverse. Pour slowly, avoid the fumes, and work in an open area. Mix in glass or enamel vessels.*
>
> *When working with acids, wear rubber gloves or use copper tongs to handle objects in the acid solution. Read the labels on chemicals to be used.*

For Cleaning Gold

Water	8 parts
Nitric acid	1 part

Use hot for best results, and handle the metal with copper tongs, or wear rubber gloves to remove the metal from the acid. Rinse carefully.

Quick-Cleaning Bright Dip

Formula #1		**Formula #2**	
Sulphuric acid	1 part	Sulphuric acid	2 parts
Nitric acid	1 part	Nitric acid	1 part

These formulas can be used on any metal but steel; they are not recommended for foils.

Acid Substitutes for Cleaning Metals

For anyone not wishing to store acids, there are products on the market such as Sparex I (for use on iron and steel), and Sparex II (for non-ferrous metals other than aluminum). There are also several cleaners on the market for use on aluminum. These products, while not as effective as acids for certain purposes, will clean the metal of oxides as is necessary before any other processes (such as enameling or antiquing) take place.

When mixing formulas containing acid, always add acid to water, never the reverse. Pour slowly, avoid the fumes, and work in an open area. Mix in glass or enamel vessels.

When working with acids, wear rubber gloves or use copper tongs to handle objects in the acid solution. Read the labels on chemicals to be used.

SURFACE CHANGES

To Frost Silver

Water	6 oz.
Sulphuric acid	1½ dr.

Add the acid to the water in an enamel or glass double boiler; heat the liquid and immerse the silver. When frosted, wash in running water and dry quickly in clean boxwood sawdust specially packed for such use.

Green on Silver

Water	1 part
Iodine crystals	1 part
Hydrochloric acid	3 parts

Dissolve the iodine crystals in the water; add the acid.

To Blacken Aluminum

There is a commercial blackener for aluminum available from the Brookstone Company (see Appendix for address), in addition to this do-it-yourself formula.

Hot water	2 qts.
Zinc chloride	1 lb.
Copper sulphate	1 oz.

Immerse metal to be blackened in the solution. To hasten the process add more copper sulphate.

> *When mixing formulas containing acid, always add acid to water, never the reverse. Pour slowly, avoid the fumes, and work in an open area. Mix in glass or enamel vessels.*
>
> *When working with acids, wear rubber gloves or use copper tongs to handle objects in the acid solution. Read the labels on chemicals to be used.*

To Whiten Brass

Water	1 qt.
Pure tin shavings	8 oz.
Cream of tartar	6 oz.

Boil the above solution; add the brass article and continue boiling until desired results are achieved.

To Color Brass

Red

Immerse brass in bright dip (see section on Pickle); then wrap in iron (wire or thin sheet), and immerse in bright dip once more. The raw red color can be modified by brushing with powdered graphite.

Bright Blue
Solution *A*

Hyposulphite of soda	½ oz.
Water	1 qt.

Dissolve the hyposulphite of soda in the water.

Solution *B*

Acetate of lead	2 oz.
Water	1 qt.

Dissolve the acetate of lead in the water. When completely dissolved, *add the lead solution to the hypo solution,* not the reverse. Bring to a boil in a double boiler and dip the brass objects in the solution. If action is too strong, add more water.

When mixing formulas containing acid, always add acid to water, never the reverse. Pour slowly, avoid the fumes, and work in an open area. Mix in glass or enamel vessels.

When working with acids, wear rubber gloves or use copper tongs to handle objects in the acid solution. Read the labels on chemicals to be used.

Dull Black on Brass

Make a strong solution of silver nitrate in one container, and nitrate of copper in another. Mix together and immerse the brass in it. Remove the brass from the solution and heat (do not rinse), until it assumes the desired color. Rinse thoroughly. (This formula is used to blacken brass used in optical instruments.)

Copper Tone on Brass

Water	2 pts.
Copper sulphate	1 tbsp.
Add sulphuric acid	½ pt.

Dissolve the copper sulphate in hot water, add the sulphuric acid. Clean the brass in bright dip (see section on Pickle), and wind with thin iron wire which will displace the copper in the copper sulphate. Place in the solution for 15 minutes, or until desired color results. Rinse thoroughly.

Browning Copper

Clean the copper in bright dip (see section on Pickle), then rub the surface with acetic acid. Place in a solution of tannic acid. The color can be controlled by heating the metal.

Two additional formulas for browning copper:

Formula #1

Potassium chlorate	1 part
Copper sulphate	1 part
Water	100 parts

When mixing formulas containing acid, always add acid to water, never the reverse. Pour slowly, avoid the fumes, and work in an open area. Mix in glass or enamel vessels.

When working with acids, wear rubber gloves or use copper tongs to handle objects in the acid solution. Read the labels on chemicals to be used.

Dissolve each chemical in water (the amount to be subtracted from the total 100 parts); combine the two solutions and add the remaining water.

Formula #2 (Dark brown on copper)

Copper sulphate	1 oz.
Hyposulphite of soda	1 oz.
Add hydrochloric acid	2 dr.

Green on Copper

Formula #1

Water	1 part
Iodine	1 part
Hydrochloric acid	3 parts

Dissolve the iodine in the water; add the acid.

Formula #2

Salt	½ oz.
Sal ammoniac	½ oz.
Ammonia	1 oz.
Vinegar	1 qt.

In separate containers, use only enough water to dissolve the salt and the sal ammoniac; combine. Add the ammonia and the vinegar. No additional water is needed.

A third alternative to produce green on copper is to steep the metal in a strong solution of salt or sal ammoniac.

COLORING EXCESS SOLDER

When soldering brass or copper it often happens that some excess soft solder shows around joints. When this occurs, the solder can be colored with a solution of copper sulphate.

When mixing formulas containing acid, always add acid to water, never the reverse. Pour slowly, avoid the fumes, and work in an open area. Mix in glass or enamel vessels.

When working with acids, wear rubber gloves or use copper tongs to handle objects in the acid solution. Read the labels on chemicals to be used.

APPENDIX

COMMERCIAL CRAFT MATERIALS AND THEIR SOURCES

MATERIALS FOR BACKING FOIL

All products in the following list are available from the Ventron Corporation, 152 Andrews St., Danvers, MA 01923. Write for catalog.

Aluminum epoxy fairing compound
Steel epoxy fairing compound
General purpose fairing compound
Aluminum epoxy, putty type
Aluminum epoxy, liquid type
Aluminum repairing compound
Lead putty
Bronze putty
Plastic steel putty
Plastic steel liquid

There are also several brands of plastic metals packed in cans and tubes that are available at hardware and department stores. Because these tend to skin over and harden quickly, it is better to thin them for application by adding acetone, available at most paint stores.

Materials of this nature are also sold in large cans for use in making metal sculptures; Sculptamold and Art-Bright are two brands sold in art stores. Lab-metal, another make, is distributed by the Brookstone Company (see Sources of Supply for address). These products cost more than the products available in hardware stores, but may be less expensive when bought in bulk.

PSEUDO-ENAMELS

In addition to enamels to be used as stiffening agents on copper foil, there are on the market today several products designed to imitate enamels, known as pseudo-enamels. Most are made of plastic and are available in paste, powder, and crystal forms.

Paste Type

Boss-Gloss comes in several colors in paste form, each jar also accompanied by a tube of hardener, to be mixed in the proportion of three parts of color to one of hardener, in the manner of epoxy compounds, which in reality this one is.

Surfaces to be decorated must be clean before the enamel is applied with a brush. It takes several hours for the Boss-Gloss to dry, and about twenty-four hours to set hard. This is an excellent substitute for vitreous enamel, with the exception that it is not as hard, nor is it scratch-free. Boss-Gloss is easiest to apply of all the substitute enamels, and it does add stiffness to foil. Available at art and craft stores, the manufacturer is California Titan Products, Santa Ana, California 92707.

Powder Type

Un-Amels come in a range of colors, and except that they are not fired in a kiln, use the same tools as those used for vitreous enameling. Powders are sifted on or applied with a spatula. They are cooked in a kitchen oven set at 350°F. When cooked, the powders fuse into a smooth surface. These are good substitutes and give added stiffness to foils.

Crystal Type

There are several makes of these plastic crystals on the market, one of which is Makit & Bakit. They are not as easy to use as the two just mentioned, but are satisfactory. They add great rigidity to foil, being more bulky than the powdered variety. They too are cooked at 350°F. in a kitchen oven.

HOT-MELT GLUE

Stick glue is loaded into an electric gun; when melted, the glue is ejected when the trigger is pulled. It sets up fast and hard, and is not too easy to manipulate, but can be smoothed with a hot soldering iron or wood-burning tool.

SOFT SOLDER

Applied over clean copper or brass foil, soft solder with flux may be used; spread with a hot soldering iron.

MOLTEN TIN

The pure metal, tin, is melted in a ladle. Copper and brass may be dipped in the molten metal and the excess shaken off. The effect is the same as a tinned copper cookpot.

CASTING RESIN

Mostly used for embedment of specimens or ornaments, casting resin (plus a few drops of hardener to cause it to set up hard) may be used as a backing for foil, or the metal may be embedded in the resin.

In addition to the products already mentioned, foil that has been modeled as a plaque to be hung may be filled before mounting with common materials such as plaster, pitch, sealing wax, and like substances. A good commercial product for this purpose is Pollyfilla, a cellulose-based repairing compound made in Canada, and available from the Ventron Corporation. (See Sources of Supply for address.)

ADHESIVES, GLUES, AND CEMENTS

Universal Glues

The best adhesive for foil workers is a universal type, good for use on almost any material. Weldbond is a fine example. Duco cement, a DuPont product, is handy for tacking foil in place, but is less strong than some of the other universal types of adhesives. Touch-N-Glue, a Weldbond product, is an excellent adhesive, and can be used in sculpture and joining seams; it is sold in hardware stores.

Epoxy Cements

Packed in two-tube kits in a variety of brands, these are good for cementing joints in foil where they meet or overlap. They are available in hardware and department stores.

Spray Glues

Spra-Ment by the 3M Company is a good adhesive for gluing foils to cardboard.

Contact Cements

Avoid the use of contact cements when possible because positioning foil before sticking is difficult; the cement grabs and holds tight. If two persons are involved, the extra pair of hands may make its use possible.

Miracle Glues

These really grab and hold, but are not easy to use. One's fingers are apt to stick together, and only acetone will free them. Being dangerous to use around children, their use is not advised.

Vinyl Paste

An adhesive used to hang vinyl wallcoverings, vinyl paste is useful for applying foil to a backing.

MISCELLANEOUS SUPPLIES

Metal Tapes

Foil may be obtained in this form, in several metals. Stainless steel tape is available in a 2-inch width and is good for covering small, round objects. It is self-adhesive. Aluminum flashing and sealing tape, .002 gauge, comes in 3-inch-by-20-foot rolls. It is useful for certain foil projects not higher than 3 inches.

Protective Sprays

There are several of these on the market, all useful for protecting metal from oxidation. Krylon is one brand. There are also silicone sprays for this purpose, available from hardware stores.

Electric Clock Movements

A battery-operated unit that measures $3^{1}/_{4}''$ x $2^{1}/_{2}''$ x $1^{3}/_{16}''$ comes complete with hands. It may be fixed to the back of a clockface with a nut that comes with it. Runs for a year when fitted with a battery (not included). Available from several mail-order houses, the Brookstone Company being one of them. (See Sources of Supply for address.)

Special Tools

National Camera and the Brookstone Company (see Sources of Supply for addresses), among others, issue catalogs containing many tools and instruments as well as workbenches that will be useful to the metalcrafter.

COMMON CHEMICALS AND THEIR SCIENTIFIC NAMES

Some formulas, particularly those from old books, use common names for chemical ingredients, therefore it is useful to know what they are in scientific terms.

Not all chemicals are dangerous, but when in doubt, they should always be handled and stored in a careful manner, and always kept out of the reach of children.

Common Name	Scientific Name
Alum	potassium aluminum sulphate
Aqua regia	a mixture of nitric and hydrochloric acids
Baking soda	sodium bicarbonate

Appendix

Figure 52. A workbench of this type is ideal, though not a necessity. Note the two working levels and many drawers.—Illustrations courtesy of National Camera, Englewood, CO.

Common Name	Scientific Name
Bluestone	copper sulphate
Blue vitriol	hydrated copper sulphate
Borax	hydrated sodium borate
Caustic potash	potassium hydroxide
Caustic soda	sodium hydroxide
Copperas	hydrated ferrous sulphate
Green vitriol	hydrated ferrous sulphide
Hartshorn	ammonium carbonate
Hypo	sodium thiosulphate

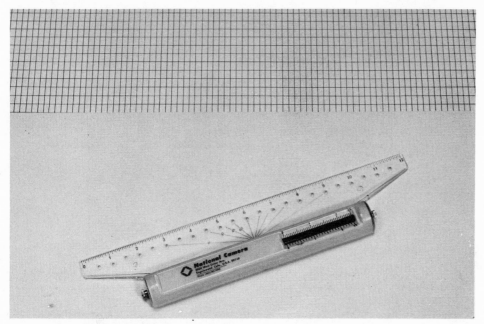

Figure 53. The Rol-Ruler is useful for ruling lines automatically.—Photograph courtesy of National Camera, Englewood, CO.

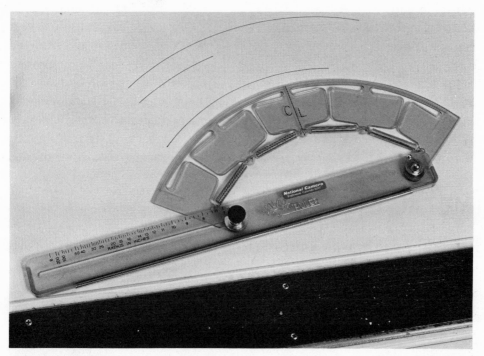

Figure 54. The Acu-Arc ruler is useful when making working drawings.—Photograph courtesy of National Camera, Englewood, CO.

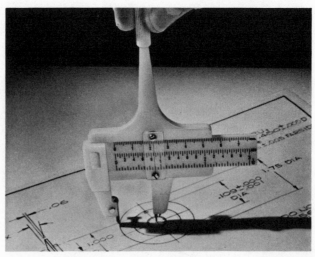

Figure 55. A new compass, Slidecomp, draws circles that are accurate within 0.005-inch.—
Photograph courtesy of Creative Instruments, Chappaqua, NY.

Common Name	*Scientific Name*
Liver of sulphur	potassium sulphide
Lye	sodium hydroxide or potassium hydroxide
Muriatic acid	hydrochloric acid
Oil of vitriol	sulphuric acid
Sal ammoniac	ammonium chloride
Salt	sodium chloride
Saltpeter	sodium nitrate or potassium nitrate
Spirits of salt	hydrochloric acid
Washing soda (sal soda)	hydrated sodium carbonate
White vitriol	zinc sulphate
Water glass	sodium silicate or potassium silicate

METAL STANDARDS

GAUGE NUMBERS AND MILLIMETER EQUIVALENTS

	American or Brown & Sharpe's	
Gauge No.	Inches	Millimeters
000000	.5800	14.732
00000	.5165	13.119
0000	.4600	11.684
000	.4096	10.404
00	.3648	9.266

Gauge No.	American or Brown & Sharpe's	
	Inches	Millimeters
0	.3249	8.252
1	.2893	7.348
2	.2576	6.543
3	.2294	5.827
4	.2043	5.189
5	.1819	4.620
6	.1620	4.115
7	.1443	3.665
8	.1285	3.264
9	.1144	2.906
10	.1019	2.588
11	.09074	2.305
12	.08081	2.053
13	.07196	1.828
14	.06408	1.628
15	.05707	1.450
16	.05082	1.291
17	.04526	1.150
18	.04030	1.024
19	.03589	.912
20*	.03196	.812
21*	.02846	.723
22*	.02535	.644
23	.02257	.573
24	.02010	.511
25†	.01790	.455
26	.01594	.405
27	.01420	.361
28	.01264	.321
29	.01126	.286
30	.01003	.255
31	.008928	.227
32	.007950	.202
33‡	.007080	.180
34‡	.006305	.160
35‡	.005615	.143
36‡	.005000	.127
37‡	.004453	.113
38‡	.003965	.101
39	.003531	.090
40	.003145	.080
41	.002800	.071
42	.002494	.063
43	.002221	.056
44	.001978	.050

*For repoussé (high relief).
†Workshop aluminum sold in hardware stores.
‡For foilcraft (low relief).

SOURCES OF SUPPLY

It would be impossible to list here all sources of supply for the craftsperson, but there are several books in print that are devoted to this subject. They are listed in the *Bibliography*.

The companies listed are some that have proven themselves as reliable.

Alpha Products- Ventron Corp. 152 Andover St. Danvers, MA 01923	Issues a catalog of an unusual assortment of tools, supplies, and chemicals, including foils and a variety of metals.
Brookstone Company Vose Farm Rd. Peterborough, NH 03458	Issues periodic catalogs of hard-to-find tools, model-maker's supplies, plastic metals, and other unusual items
National Camera 2000 West Union Ave. Englewood, CA 80110	Issues a catalog of hard-to-find tools for fine work, and a wide variety of supplies useful to craftspersons
Macmillan Arts and Crafts, Inc. 9520 Baltimore Ave. College Park, MD 20740	Issues a catalog of fine art and craft supplies, including foils and enamels
Nasco Arts and Crafts Fort Atkinson, WI 53538	Issues a catalog of art and craft supplies, including kilns and enameling supplies
U.S. General Supply Corp. 100 General Pl. Jericho, NY 11753	Issues a catalog of tools at discount prices including welding and soldering supplies and power tools, including a gasket cutter useful for cutting circles in foil
S and S Arts and Crafts Colchester, CT 06611	Issues a catalog of craft supplies useful to the foil worker and sculptor
Koenig Art Shop, Inc. 166 Fairfield Ave. Bridgeport, CT 06611	Art supplies, including Krylon and Illinois Bronze spray paints. Write for price list

Allcraft Tool and Supply Co. 20 West 48th St. New York, NY 10036	Issues a catalog of tools and materials for most crafts; jewelry supplies & findings
C. R. Hill Company 35 West Grand River Detroit, MI 48226	Foils in most metals in bulk are available. Write for information
Revere Copper and Brass Co. 196 Diamond St. Brooklyn, NY 11222	Metal supplies, including Britannia metal and pewter foils. Write for names of retail outlets.
Handy and Harmon 850 Third Ave. New York, NY 10022	Foils in precious metals; write for information
Aiko's 714 North Wabash Chicago, IL 60611	Papers in wide variety suitable for paper sculpture and decorative purposes. Write for information
Art Foam 100 E. Montauk Hwy. Lindenhurst, NY 17557	Urethane foam in blocks, suitable for making armatures for foil metal sculptures. Write for catalog.
American Handicrafts Outlets in most cities; check the telephone directory for the nearest one or write to: Tandycrafts 3 Tandy Center Ft. Worth, TX 76102	Issues a catalog listing supplies for a wide variety of crafts

BIBLIOGRAPHY

Alkema, Chester Jay. *Creative Paper Crafts.* New York: Sterling Publishing Co., 1967.
A helpful book for the worker in foils interested in sculpture.

Aspden, George. *Model Making in Paper, Cardboard and Metal.* London: Studio Vista, 1964.
An excellent book on the subject, which can be helpful to the foil worker.

Bergsøe, Paul. *The Metallurgy and Technology of Gold and Platinum Among the Pre-Columbian Indians.* København: Danmarks Naturvidenskabelige Samfund, 1937.
Rare out of print booklet describing the exceedingly rare skills in metalworking of the Indians of Central America, as revealed by excavations of known sites. Worth studying if a copy can be found.

Clarke, Carl Dame. *Molding and Casting.* 2nd edition. Butler, Maryland: The Standard Arts Press, 1949.
The bible on ways and means to make plaster and other types of casts. Useful to many craftspersons.

Collier, Graham. *Form, Space, and Vision.* Englewood Cliffs, N.J.: Prentice-Hall, 1972.
Sources of inspiration useful to the designer.

Coxeter, H. M. S. *Regular Polytopes.* New York: Dover Publications, 1973.
A fascinating book for those interested in geometric solids and their development.

De La Iglesia, Maria Elenda. *The New Catalogue of Catalogues.* New York: Random House, 1972.
A complete guide to shopping by mail worldwide. A handy reference work.

deLemos, Pedro. *Creative Art Crafts.* Books 1 and 2. Worcester, Mass.: Davis Press.
An inspirational book with chapters on working with metal foils featured in both books.

Estrin, Michael. *2,000 Designs, Forms and Ornaments.* New York: William Penn Publishing Co., 1947.
Just what the title indicates.

French, Thomas E., and Vierck, Charles J. *Engineering Drawing & Graphic Technology,* 11th edition. New York: McGraw-Hill, 1972.

Glassman, Judith. *National Guide to Craft Supplies.* New York: Van Nostrand Reinhold Co., 1975.
Advertised as the "Yellow Pages for the crafts." A very useful book for the craftsperson.

Haeckel, Ernst. *Art Forms in Nature.* New York: Dover Publications, 1974.
An inspirational book for the designer. Well illustrated.

Hornung, Clarence Pearson. *Treasury of American Design.* Two volumes. New York: H. N. Abrams, 1972.
A fertile source for the designer who likes Americana. Beautifully illustrated with many color plates.

Howlett, Carolyn S. *Art in Craftmaking.* New York: Van Nostrand Reinhold Co., 1974.
A stimulating book full of ideas and new approaches to old crafts.

Knoblaugh, Ralph R. *Model Making for Industrial Design.* New York: McGraw-Hill Book Co., 1958.
A useful book for craftspersons.

Maryon, Herbert. *Metalwork and Enamelling.* 4th edition. New York: Dover Publications, 1971.
The standard work of reference on the coloring and finishing of metals, containing useful tables, standards, and detailed information on metalworking in general.

Meyer, Franz S. *Handbook of Ornament.* 4th edition. New York: Dover Publications, 1892.

Over 3000 illustrations of styles of ornament from the past. A good reference work.

Newman, James R. *The World of Mathematics.* Four volumes. New York: Simon and Schuster, 1956.
A refresher course for those who have forgotten their schooling in mathematics. Has material on geometry in the arts.

Osburn, Paul Neff. *Pewter—Spun, Wrought and Cast.* Scranton: International Text Book Co., 1935.
A well-illustrated, step-by-step manual on the craft of spinning metal.

Reagan, J. E., and Smith, E. E. *Metal Spinning.* Milwaukee: Bruce Publishing Co., 1936.
A good instruction book on this craft.

Rosenbloom, Joseph. *Craft Supplies Supermarket.* Willits, California: Oliver Press (Charles Scribner's Sons), 1974.
A directory of supplies, materials, tools, and equipment for almost every craft and hobby.

Speltz, Alexander. *Styles of Ornament.* New York: Grosset & Dunlap, 1936.
One of the standard works on the origin of design, and its development through the ages. (Reprinted by Dover Publications, N.Y.)

Thomajan, P. K. *Handbook of Designs and Motifs.* New York: Tudor Publishing Co., 1950.
Offers a wide variety of designs from traditional and oriental sources.

Yamada, Sadami, Kiyotada, and Ito. *New Dimensions in Paper Craft.* Tokyo: Japan Publications Trading Co., 1966.
A valuable book on the crafts of paper folding and sculpture, helpful to the foil worker who attempts sculpture in this medium.

INDEX